Life Lessons of a Novice Rider

By Robin Olivero

Designed by Sarah C. Stegall

LIFE LESSONS OF A NOVICE RIDER

Design by Sarah C. Stegall. sarahstegalls@gmail.com

Acknowledgment

There were very few who knew of this endeavor, but I would be remiss to not extend my thanks and gratitude for their encouragement. Sometimes their seemingly small words of encouragement made the biggest difference in not just seeing this as a silly idea and keeping it stored away with my many other journal entries. Thank you to those who took the time to spur me on; your encouragement is greatly appreciated.

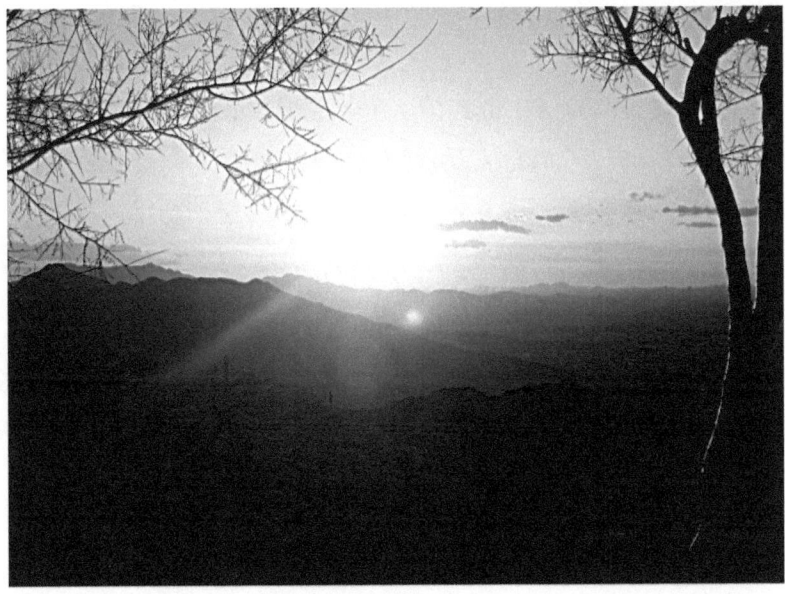

"It is not until we see ourselves with eyes wide open and heart unguarded that we are ready to accept who we are and become who we are created to be. I have learned more about myself through the journey with my horse, than with the people in my life. With people you learn who they are, with your horse, you are confronted with who you are."

~ Robin Olivero

Forward

When I moved from Illinois to Arizona my life completely changed. The way of life here is so different from the fast-paced business world by day and small town everyone knows everyone's business by night life in Illinois. The pace is slower, but not at a stand-still and though people are friendly and kind, they don't know or gossip about each other. The scenery is not a concrete jungle or flat land with local shopping malls; it's open, mountainous and like something out of a John Wayne movie. Horses are a part of everyday life in Arizona like little dogs are a part of 9 out of 10 families in Illinois.

I have always loved horses and as far back as my Marble the Mustang on wheels, I have wanted a horse. I didn't move to Arizona because I wanted a horse; it just felt like home the first time I visited, despite the miles it put between me and all those I know and love. However, one of the best parts of moving here has been my horse Jr. My lifestyle has changed so much that telling you all about the life I am making for myself out here and the occasional pictures I text, you really couldn't imagine just how much things have changed for me.

One other love I have always had is a love for writing. One day I wrote and posted on Facebook a silly little paragraph comparing a recent horseback ride to life. The response was lighthearted and encouraging. While sharing this with my dear friend, horse and ranch owner, Terri, she strongly encouraged me to send this in to a magazine and continue writing. I didn't submit this anywhere, but I did continue writing. As I shared these stories with Terri, she relentlessly encouraged me to do something with them. Hence, you are now reading Life Lessons of a Novice Rider, a compilation of some of the most memorable first-year moments I've had with my horse that have also made me reflect on my life. I'm not looking at publishing this or becoming an actual legitimate author, but rather wanted to share some of my deepest reflections with my family and closest friends.

The writing may not be Pulitzer Prize winning, but it is written with a genuine attempt to welcome you into my world beyond the surface of what friends and even family usually see. I hope you find enjoyment in reading and think of me when you do.

A Gift Horse

Jr is boarded at the ranch of a dear friend of mine, Terri. When I first met Terri we hit it off instantly. Her love for all animals is unparalleled to anyone I know and her knowledge about animals is second only to her instincts about them. Terri has several animals; when I first began my western girl adventures on her ranch, she had 17 critters-4 horses, 4 dogs, 5 cats, 2 goats, a pony and a midget mule! There will be more about them later. It all started when I helped a friend of a friend of hers care for the animals when Terri was away for a few days. I simply wanted to be around the animals so I offered to help. After the first time I went, I never stopped going. I didn't actually meet Terri until about a month after I had been coming to her house. I didn't want anything from her, I just wanted to be around her "family" so I would show up, clean stalls; clean water buckets, give them water, whatever needed to be done. I would groom them and give them treats (horse cookies), that was my reward and I loved it! Terri would constantly thank me over and over; it took her a while to realize I genuinely just love animals and being there was a blessing for me.

After a couple of months and realizing I wasn't going anywhere, Terri suggested I take on a project horse: Jr. She said since I was going to be around and I wanted to learn, I could work with him. I was thrilled to have an opportunity to learn under her. She has taught me so much-from saddling up to cleaning his "frogs" and how to actually "work" with a horse to break some of their bad behaviors. I knew at some point I would be getting my own horse and boarding him there; Terri, out of kindness, took a lot of her valuable time to teach me. I had figured after about a year I would be ready to take on the feat of horse ownership and was soaking up everything I could in preparation.

Jr had been acting up and his barn sour behavior had Terri contemplating finding him a new home; I was indifferent to the whole idea, but he was her horse. Despite initially being more drawn to her other gelding Leroy, I had come to love Jr, but him being her horse I wouldn't of argued with her, well, so I thought. Then one day Terri and I were cleaning stalls, and she said "I know you didn't want to own a horse yet, but when you are ready, would you consider Jr?" Knowing she thought about selling him and having invested the time into him I had already, Jr and I bonded; I immediately said, "Oh no, please don't sell him, I will find a way to buy him from you." She just smiled and told me she's not selling him, she is giving him to me. I just kind of stood there in utter shock and amazement that she just gave me a horse, and not just any horse-Jr. Long story short, of course I accepted him and thanked her, but it took me about a month and a half for it to sink in. At that point, while were cleaning stalls again, I sincerely thanked her with the deepest sense of appreciation I had within me, and then there we were standing in horse poop holding rakes, hugging and crying.

I don't know why it was so hard for me to accept Jr; I mean, I did say thank you initially, but it took quite a few weeks for the magnitude of what she did to sink in. Terri doesn't just give away animals to anyone, when she finds them a home the person must meet her standards. The giving of Jr to me spoke highly of her perception of me; that was difficult to process. I didn't know how to receive this precious gift horse and thank you just didn't seem like enough. Being one who likes to give without expecting in return, I had to simply accept and say thank you, as I do understand receptivity of someone's selfless giving is a gift and blessing in return to them. I am so glad I didn't "look a gift horse in the mouth" and refuse her heartfelt gesture; I cannot imagine my life without all the joy, life lessons and memories that gift horse has given me.

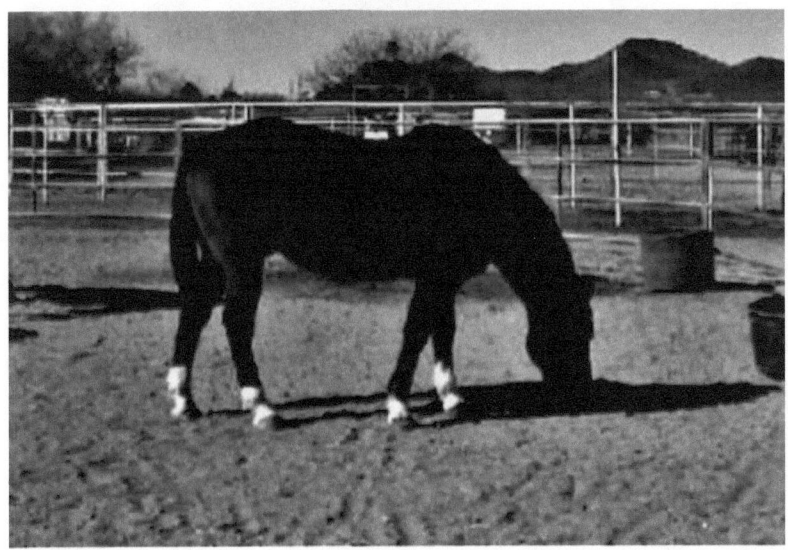

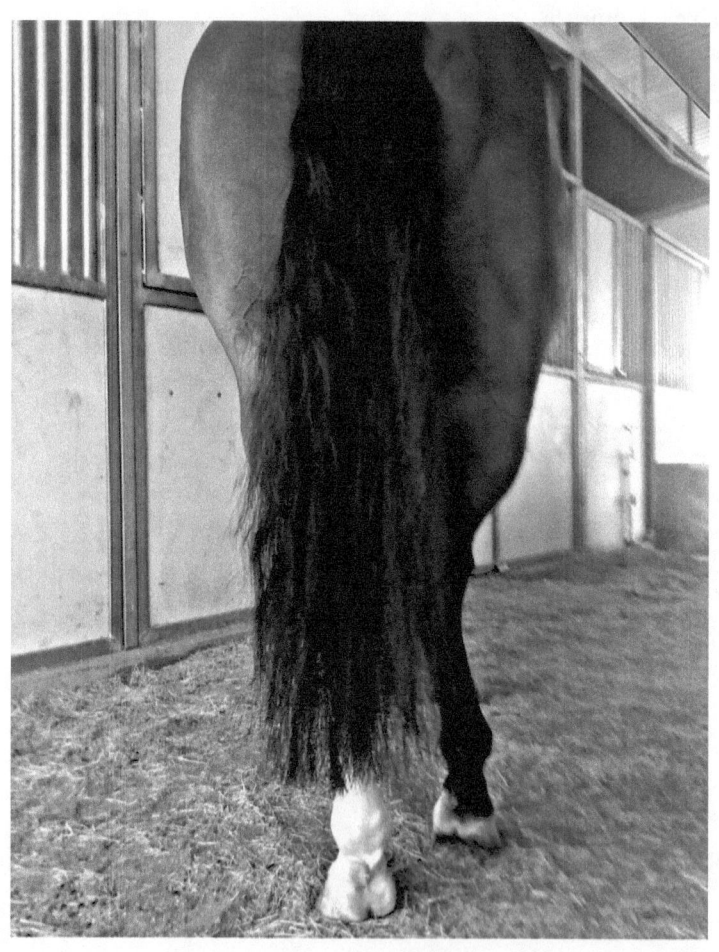

A Good Swift Kick in the Ass

Jr is 19, which in horse years really isn't all that old, but also doesn't make him a spring chicken either. One hot summer morning, a group of us took all the horses out for a ride to visit a friend's ranch who boards Arabian and Quarter horses. It was about a forty minute ride by horse with Leroy, Cali, Filly, and my Jr. While visiting, we tied up our horse and checked out all the boarded horses on this ranch. It was amazing to see these beautiful, almost royal horses with their braided manes and tails move about the ranch. The male horses, Jr and Leroy, weren't taking too well to this. Jr was very agitated and was causing quite a ruckus in his little area. Leroy broke out in a sweat so bad we had to hose him off. Eventually we hit the path back and made it home where everyone but Jr was released in the arena to roll, be hosed down and put in their stalls for the day. Jr, however, was kept saddled until my friend's 9 year old daughter came by to ride him, as it was her first encounter with a real horse. It was pretty hot out. Jr had a long morning ride, but I knew he would handle it patiently and gentling, as this is my gentle giant's personality. While waiting, I rode him in the arena for bit, taking him through barrels and just having fun. My friend arrived and her little girl's first ride went great! Finally it was time to let Jr rest after taking his saddle off, letting him roll and being hosed down. When it came to for him to roll, I was expecting him to do as he usually does; roll on one side, pop back up, then roll on the other. That day was a little different; Jr rolled and seemed quite happy, but then he didn't pop back up, he just laid there. I got closer to him, touched his face, looked in his eyes, and he just looked back and didn't move. My heart stopped; my eyes welled up with tears as I felt helpless. "What is wrong with my baby? Get up, please just get up…" He wouldn't move, he just stared back at me kind of dazed. I looked over at Terri across the arena and called out to her. She hollered back "I'm watching him" and she sounded a little concerned as well. Her boyfriend came out towards us and told me to step back. He gave him a good swift kick in the ass and pushed him up on his feet. Jr was a little slow getting going, but then he walked around a bit. This happened with him one other time. We're not sure why, but it would seem he was just tired.

I imagine you get the point without needing me to expound. It's unfortunate but the reality is that sometimes we all need a good swift kick in the ass to get up on our feet and start moving. It's unfortunate that sometimes pain needs to be a motivating force, but I guess until it hurts we don't realize the importance of mobility.

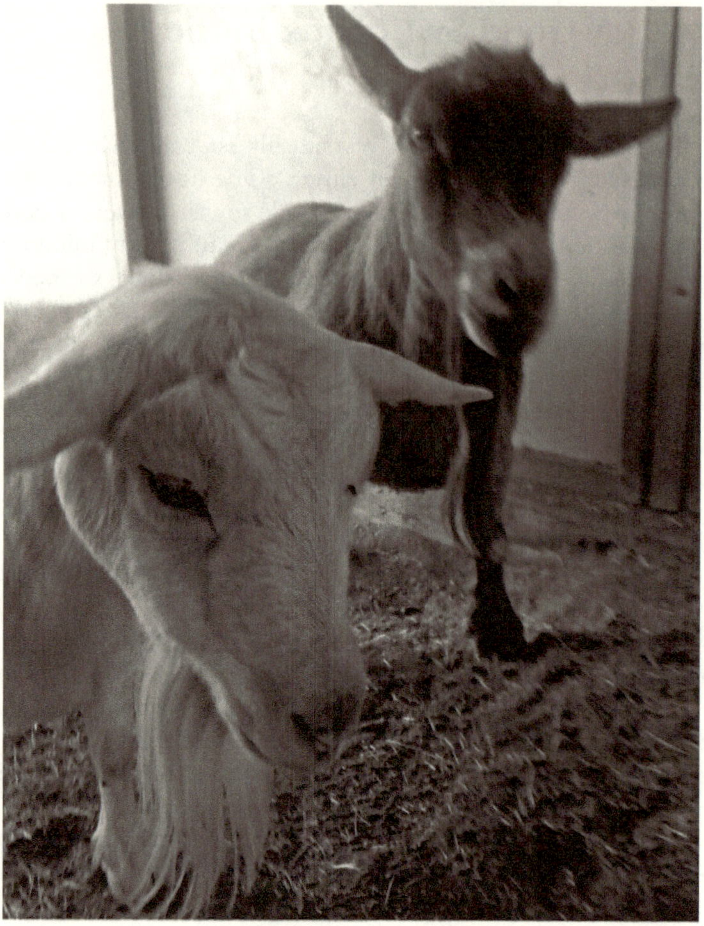

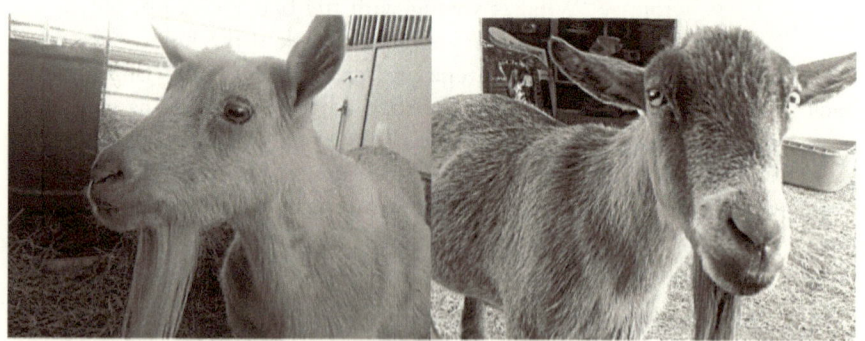

Almond Butter

There are two silly goats that roam the ranch, Almond is the white goat, and Butter is brown. Goats are the funniest little animals; they are not very vocal and scare quite easily. Their little feet move so fast when they try to escape perceived danger yet they don't get very far very fast. When you scratch their heads or necks they just freeze and almost look hypnotized. They don't cause any real trouble or get in the way; they aren't trained to do any fancy tricks and really, they kind of seem to enjoy hanging out all day. Their faces are funny and their eyes seem to always have this odd my brain is thinking too hard look. Almond and Butter are very silly goats who seem to just enjoy being…that's it, just being. They have no real needs other than food and water; they don't need attention, but will take it when you give it. They are simply just content for the moment.

Content for the moment, how nice is that? I find moments of contentment are necessary for life long sanity. Unlike goats though, we do have reason for concern and the planning of important life events. Yet interestingly, when we become consumed with these busy, hustle, bustle moments, we miss the contentment that allows us opportunities to be grateful and cherish all the good in life we do have. Those moments when everything just stops around us and we can inventory how blessed we really are; moments of serenity when you can see how simple attaining peace can be, that it actually dwells within you. Since I have lived in Arizona, I have taken many moments to take a walk or drive to a distance beautiful place and just take in the moment…like a silly little goat. Those moments have been protected by turning off the cell phone, not bringing the computer and surrounding myself with the beauty of what has been given to me by God and not fabricated by man. Taking time for yourself is not selfish; it is necessary. It renews your energy, clears your mind and prioritizes the disheveled mess of the lives we live. So if you call one day and the phone goes right to voice mail, I am working on my sanity…Don't take it personal, leave a message and I will get back to you.

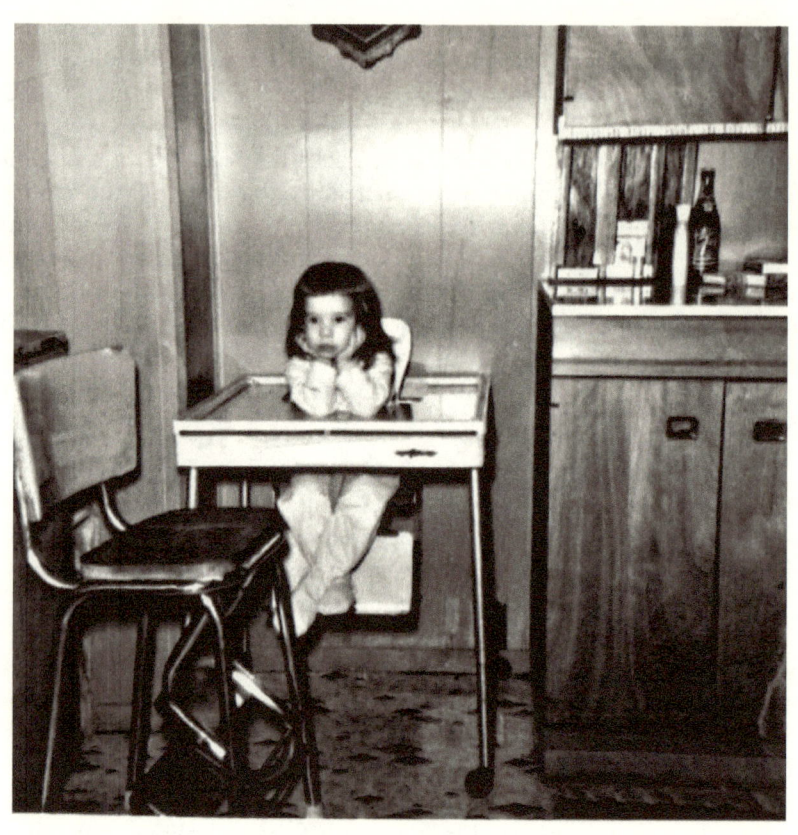

Back To Where You Came From

Snickers is a sweet horse but a temporary family member. I resisted getting too close to him because he wasn't one of Terri or my horses and the odds were he wouldn't be there long. Yet there was a part of me that couldn't resist. Snickers had issues...medically speaking. He came from a family who gave him away for no apparent reason. He's beautiful, big and sweet. Unfortunately, we came to discover that he's lame. Between Terri, her boyfriend and my combined time and money, it just wouldn't be enough to give him what he needs to be happy, healthy, and have all his needs met. With that, Snickers must go back to where he came from.

Sometimes I think about where I came from; despite any of the hard knocks and hard to imagine moments, I am here today reasonably happy, healthy and have my needs met. It's important to not gaze to long into the past, but sometimes reflecting can create a sense of appreciation for how far you've come. I have no desire to go back to where I came from; visiting on occasion is plenty enough. When I think about Snickers I'm thankful I have a choice. Snickers will, unfortunately, have to hope for another opportunity to find a good life. Me on the other hand, I have been given the chance to embrace it. While he will still be lame and stuck back where he came from, I can, even emotionally and mentally lame at times, choose to not go backwards and make the most of once-in-a-lifetime opportunities. I have found the most precious gift we have been given in this life is the ability to choose and the wisest choices are simply those that are made without regret.

Buck Off

As a novice rider, one thing I have feared is being bucked off. I've been on many recreational rides over the years and always managed to stay on when things got rough. However, I hear, as a serious rider and horse owner, a good buck off is inevitable. So what do you do when you are doing everything right but you experience the big "BUCK YOU"? When my sweet barn-sour baby suddenly became my persistently, surprisingly, overly agitated buckaroo, I did all the things I had been taught: remain calm (yeah right), turn him in a tight circle, stop him, calm him, step him back and then move forward. Do not let him get the best of you, or he will continue with the same bad behavior every time he doesn't want to do what you want. I was even advised to spur him on and let him run it off. Well, not with me on him! I'm adventurous; I am not stupid. Unfortunately, after several bucking fits in attempt to involuntarily dismount me, I calmed us both down, voluntarily dismounted my horse (feet first) and led him closer to home before trying again. The walk back was more of an attitude adjustment time for me and my boy, but we managed. Before he was able to settle in for the night, we spent a lot more time together working on HIS attitude. His attitude? It's interesting to me that people say your horse is a reflection of you. If that be true, how do you process the moment when your usually calm, compliant horse turns into a bucking hell on four legs? When all things are in check: saddle, reins, stirrups, clean frogs, bit, non-threatening environment, the problem is obviously internal and there is just no excuse or justification for that behavior. Just like life when it gives you the boot, take a look behind that stunning, "fake it till you make it" smile you wear and stop making excuse, justifying your circumstances and be honest about what the real problem is; chances are it's you. Ouch…yeah, who said being BUCKED wasn't supposed to hurt? Get back up, shake off the dust and get back in the saddle.

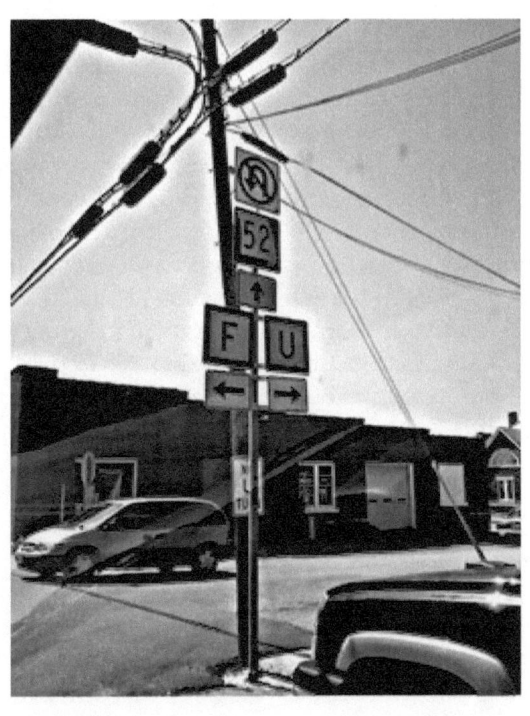

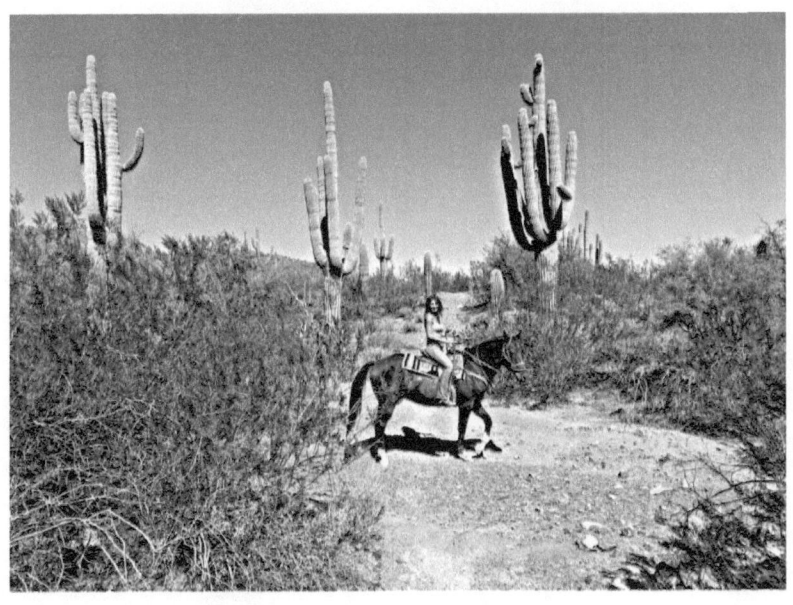

Barn Sour

After my first serious bucking adventure, getting back in the saddle and hitting the "bucking trail" it happened on was very unnerving. I was fine preparing my horse, working him in the arena and heading out to the trail. Then, for what seems like an obvious reason, as soon as we hit the sandy path, my heart started pounding and every little move Jr (my horse) made out of step with a steady walk made my stomach turn. I wanted to turn around and go back home. Oh no! It's happening! I'm becoming my horse! I'm turning barn sour! I laugh about it now; in less than a week, I went from learning, and growing slightly past novice rider, to a frightened child on her first pony ride. All I could think about was getting back home without being bucked. We made it just fine; it was actually a nice ride, but one where I had to let go of my fear and allow myself to trust him a little. I've heard riding is about mutual trust; I am learning this to be true. Despite maintaining control, when you've been hurt, relinquishing that control can be very scary. We all feel the sting of pain, regret or tragedy, and fear follows these inevitable events the next time we encounter a familiar feeling that brought those events to pass. Like riding, we can be afraid, very afraid, but the key is to not be paralyzed by that fear or worse, revert to behaviors that perpetuate stagnation. Fear can either make you wiser or barn sour. It is foolish to think I will never ride Jr again. Like life; he is imperfect, but, as scary as maybe reliving an unpleasant moment is and experiencing what good can come by confronting your fear, you will find the outcome far outweighs the risk…and gets you out of the barn.

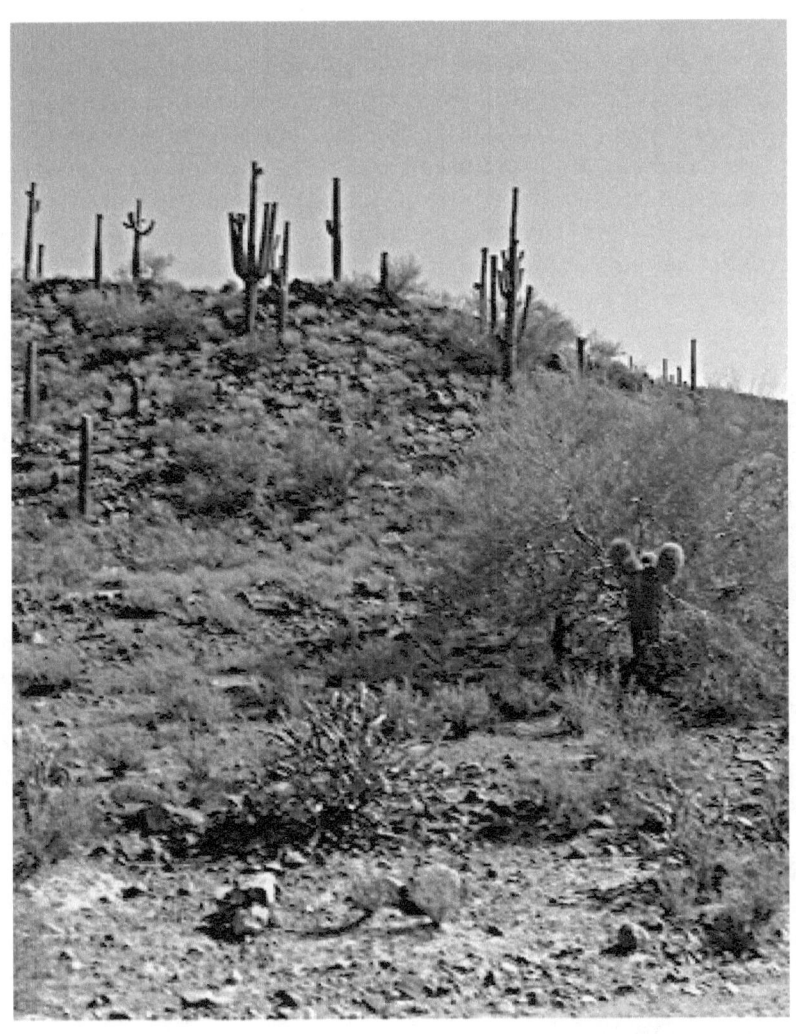

Be Free

The ranch is set up with stables and stalls nicely laid out with two on one side and two across a breezeway with the tack room and hay room between each pair of stalls. There are a two outdoor stalls and an arena. The arena is rather large and used for running the horses, working with them and allowing them space to just roam around with boundaries to prevent them from roaming around the ranch freely. The arena boundaries and stall barriers are designed to keep the horses safe from the elements outside like the heat of the day, any human things placed in those areas that could hurt them and basically just provide a good guideline as to where to go and not go for their own good. On occasion the horses find a way to escape those boundaries; some can function fine, others not so good. Once Leroy got out of his stall and just ran around crazy! He was difficult to catch and boy, did he get a talking to after that! On the other hand, Jr, the older, more life-experienced horse got out and kind of checked things out. He went stall to stall saying hi to everyone, and it was a pretty uneventful adventure. I guess horses like to be free and test those boundaries just like we do.

Being free is it a gift or earned? Is it innate or learned? When taking a panoramic view of the ranch and envisioning the horses getting out, it's humorous, though dangerous. The horses don't really fight to get out of their stalls; they are actually pretty content in there. Yet given the opportunity to roam freely, they take it. Looking back panoramically over my life, I realize that freedom is a matter of perspective and boundaries are healthy. I have always taught my kids the importance of choice and consequence. Every big or little decision you make must carefully be made with the outcome in mind. Can you live with it with for the rest of your life? I'd like to be careful in explaining that I mean "in your mind." When you look in the mirror; can you face yourself with that decision? We are all free; we are free to choose, decide and create boundaries that protect us. When we allow others to determine our boundaries and influence our decisions, we have willfully forfeited our freedom. When this happens, we can play the martyr. That it wasn't/isn't in our control and in misery, complain about being stuck in a less than satisfying unhappy life. The reality is we are free to change, create, shape, determine, and direct our own lives. Our circumstances may not be the best, but the boundaries we place in our lives will determine the level of freedom we live with. Just like Leroy and Jr, freedom can be a blessing or lesson. Really, it all depends on what you do with it.

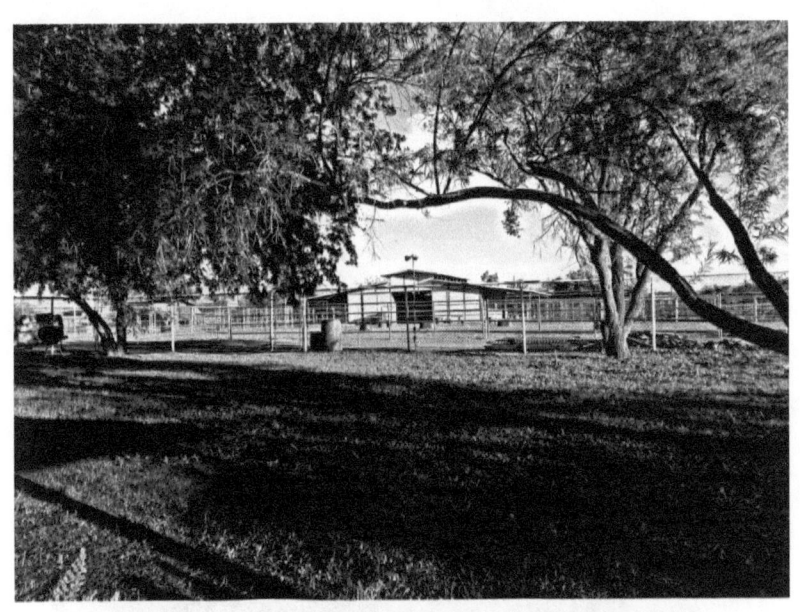

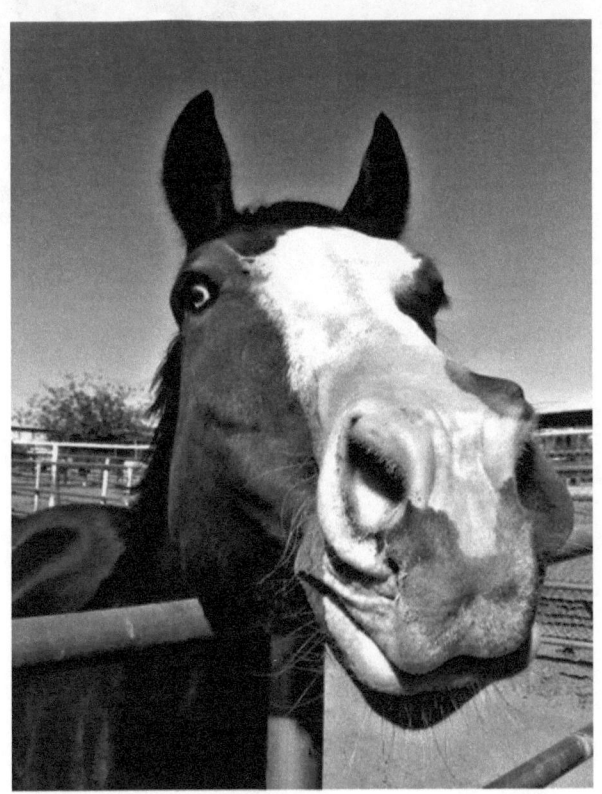

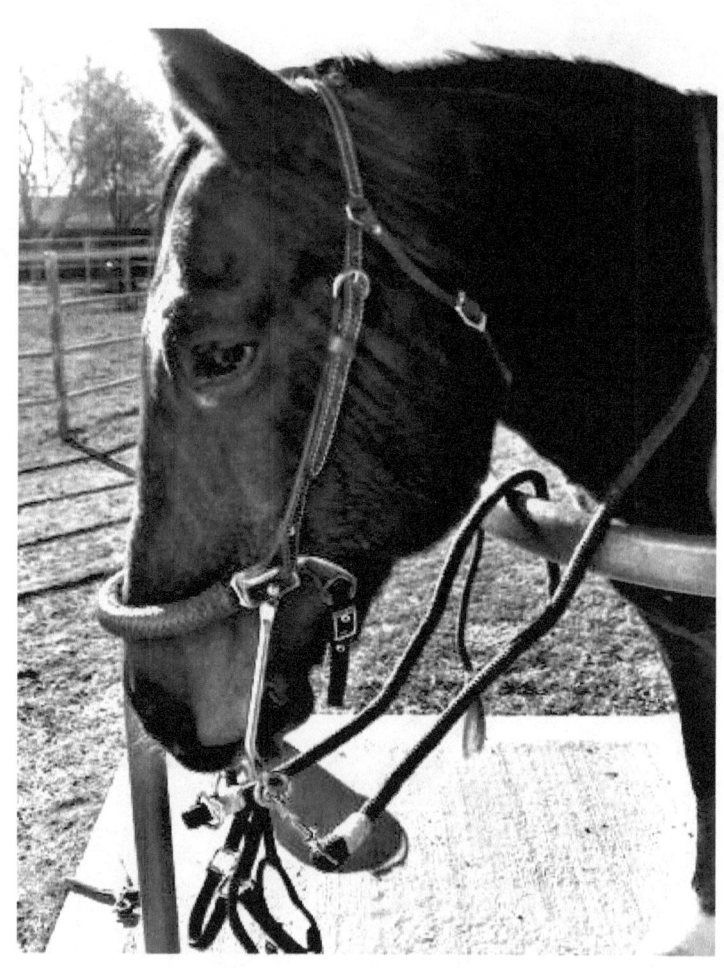

For God's Sake...Don't Look Back!

As a novice rider, I am learning something with every ride. Having a barn-sour horse, I have learned when I look forward to where I want my horse to take me and keep his reins aligned with that direction, there is little resistance and we get there without fighting each other for the route we want to take. When distractions arise in his peripheral vision, I have to maintain our focus with a little reminder to stay focused on our destination. When I become distracted and for whatever reason, look behind me while moving forward, despite my best efforts, with the slightest shift in the reins or unintentional tap with my foot from looking back, he follows my signal and we're changing directions. Before you know it, he's heading back home, and I'm having to exert a lot of effort, turn him in circles a few times and bring him back to moving forward. Interesting how life is like riding: pick your destination, don't lose sight of where you're going, keep distractions from shifting your direction and for God's sake...don't look back!

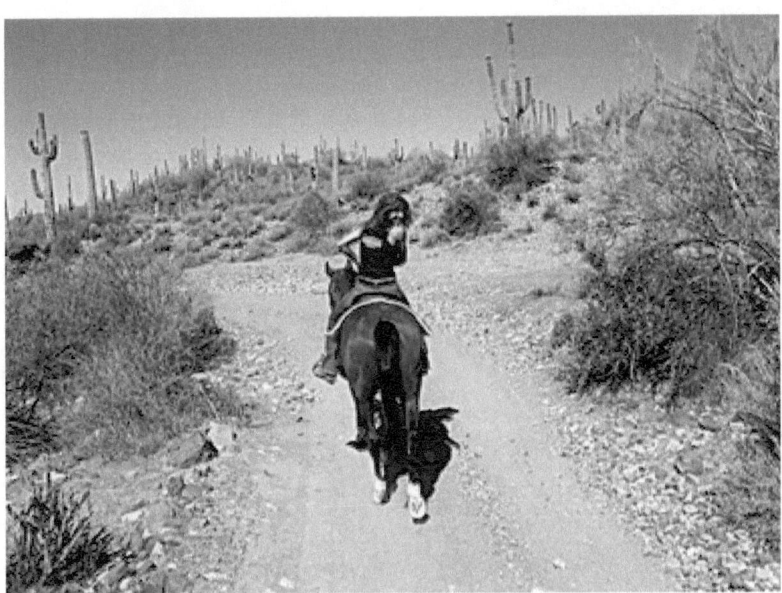

Goodbye Gus

Gus was the midget mule of the gang. He was the cutest short, fat, bouncy little mule who just meandered around the ranch. He came with "Pony" and they stuck together pretty much most of the time. Gus would come up to you and given his height, would rub his nose up and down your upper thigh, hitting your lower butt check. He was so doggone cute, you would just stand there and giggle because he was so silly. He was lovable and just moved around the grounds happily without a real care in the world. He had thyroid issues which made him over weight, but that never stopped him from pretty much doing anything. It was hard to say goodbye to Gus; he was old and though it was just his time, it was sad to think of life on the ranch without him.

Saying goodbye to someone you love is never easy. When their life leaves an indelible impression upon the unseen elements of your life, that mark left almost leaves a dent, though upon the intangible, that can hurt worse than a cut, scrape or bruise, even worse than a broken bone. The word "goodbye" is a shortened version of the term "God be with you", which I find a little more palatable as goodbye is just so final. There is just nothing pleasant about goodbye unless it's "good riddance", which is "a pleasure to be rid of." So how do we cope with the "goodbye" due to a loss, as well as, that dent left by what once impressed upon your inner most being. I really don't have an answer, twelve step plan or grand revelation. I only know some pain just doesn't go away, and we learn, through whatever means necessary, to just adjust. That dent may never be grown back over, and we may be all bumpy inside, but somehow we all manage to get through. I once read a wise saying I will leave you with… "I may not get over it, but I will get through it." Sounds a lot like the first step is acceptance for what is and to take every step thereafter like it is your first step. Eventually, I suppose we move forward and find ourselves some place we never thought we'd be…on the other side of the first step.

Goodbye Gus ole pal, you are missed.

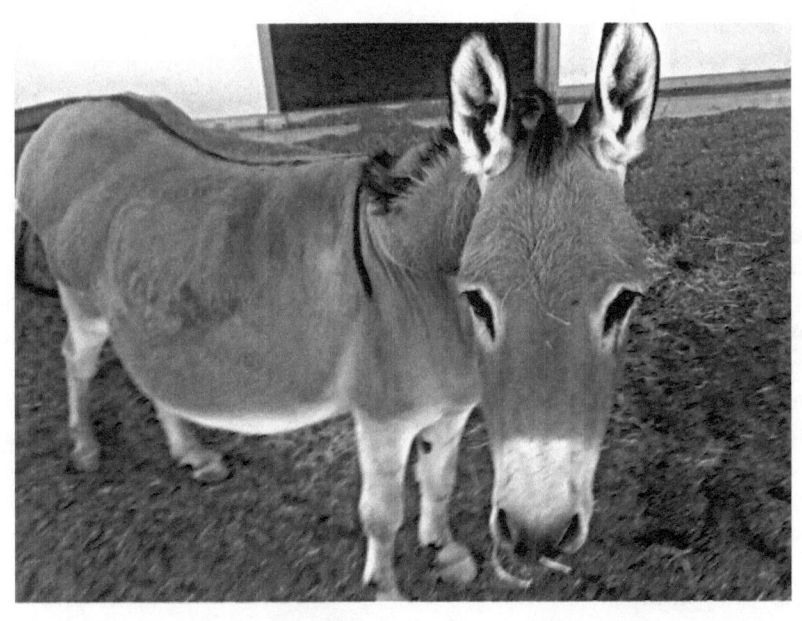

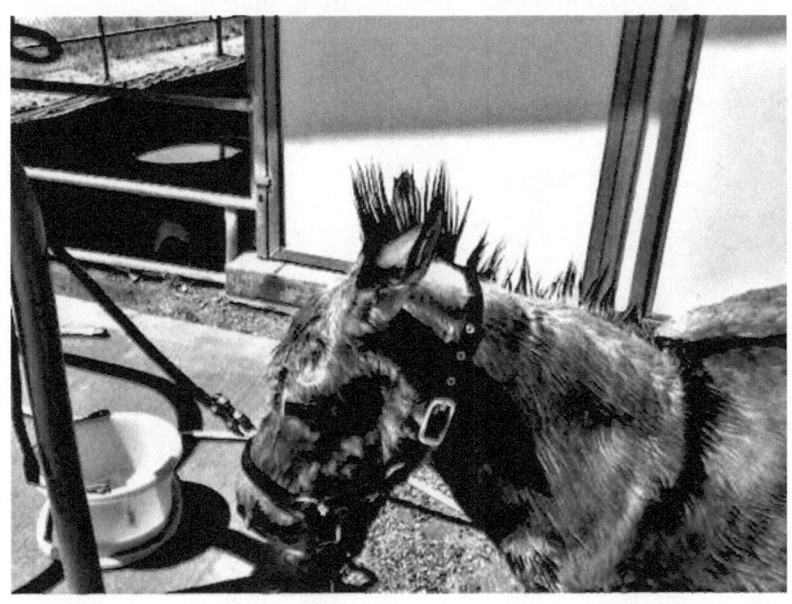

HAY!!!!

Feed time is an interesting point in the day with horses. You become the most loved, cherished human being on the planet when your presence is accompanied by a flake of hay. Just the sound of the door opening to grab hay and all the horses' ears perk up, their heads turn and their attention is fix...on hay. Hay? Dried grass compacted into a neat little pile hay? Yes, hay. I define hay as that dry, itchy stuff that finds its way deep into the crevices tucked neatly under my shirt; down my front, down my back, on my arms, in my boots, and though I am not sure how it happens, even down my jeans. I, unlike horses, do not get that warm "I am oh so happy" feeling about hay. Though I must say, despite the ramifications of my servitude, it truly is a joy seeing these big critters' excitement about the whole thing. (Even now I feel a little itchy reminiscing about feed time). No matter what they are doing, once they hear, see or smell hay, they have the unwavering pursuit of consumption of that hay and once they are indulging full face in it, they are content and happy. Typically after feeding, I just sit back and watch them with a big smile because they are happy. Isn't that the way it should be when you love someone? Shouldn't we find pleasure in their happiness? Odd as it is, that hay disrupts my peaceful little world with irritating fits of scratching. It is well worth the non-life altering moment of my discontent just to see my boy and his buddies happy.

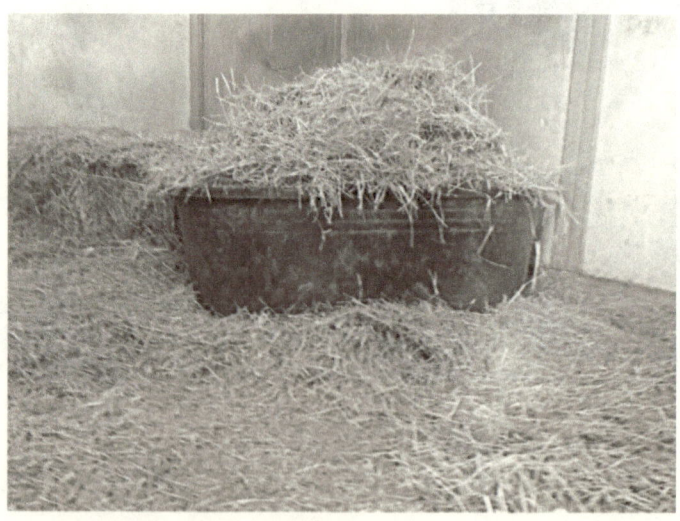

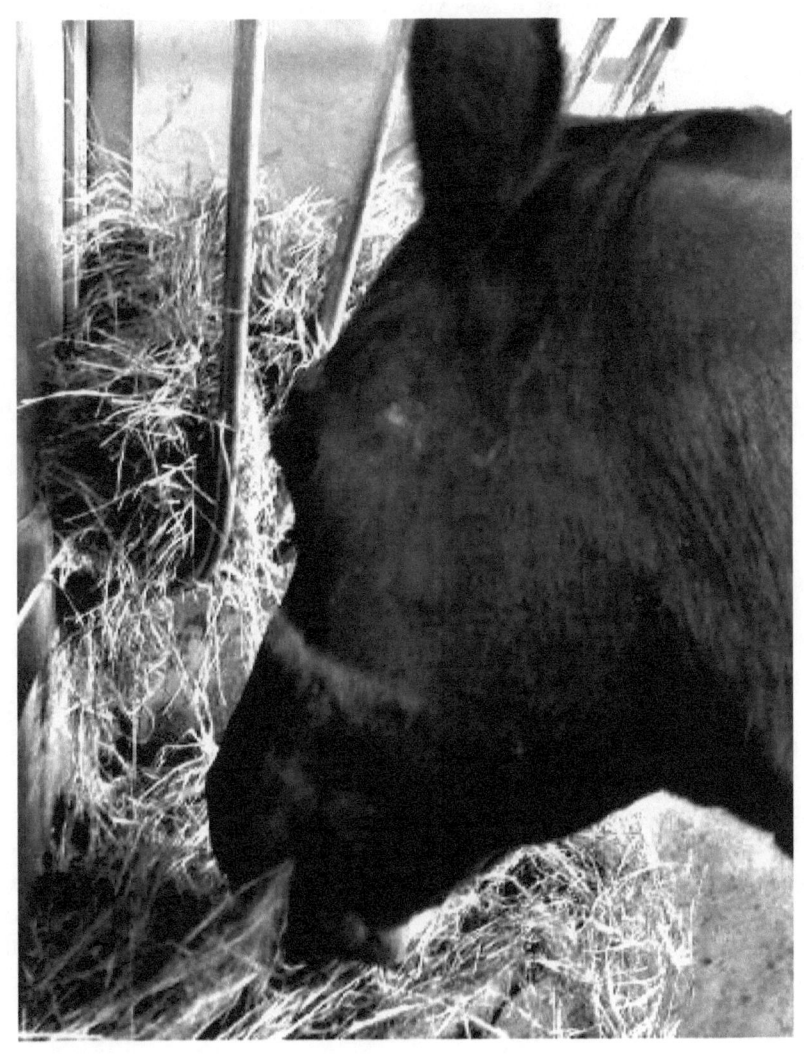

In or Out

Leroy is the class clown. He is the youngest of all the gang and has a personality that just makes you laugh by simply looking at him. He has a big face, a "crazy" eye (one blue, one brown) and a very thick mane and tale. Leroy is the one who ate part of the interior on my car door when I parked a little too close to the arena. Leroy likes to play and seems to get into mischief when left to himself. One of the funniest things he does is open and close the inside stall door. It is the craziest thing. One day I arrived at the ranch and did my typical rounds with cookies; every horse gets a hug and treat hello. Leroy was just hanging in this stall and happy to receive his treat. About 20 minutes later I keep hearing a loud banging and for the life of me, couldn't figure out what the heck was going on. I looked in all the stalls and everything looked ok. BANG! BANG! BANG! What the heck is that damn noise? Finally, I go into Leroy's stall and didn't see him. I briefly panicked until I realize the inside stall door is closed and he was on the other side. Leroy then opens the door and sticks his head through it with an almost "Peek-a-boo" look. All I could do is laugh.

As a kid, mom would often times yell at us "IN OR OUT!" because we girls had a bad habit of trying to orchestrate temperature control for our neighborhood. At least that was mom's perception. "We're not heating the whole neighborhood, close the door!" or "In or out! We're not paying for the neighborhood to enjoy our A/C." In or out… interesting concept. In Leroy's case, he was just bored and wanted to play. For us, I wonder why we find it so hard to figure out doors and their use. Sometimes we open doors we shouldn't and shut doors…all out SLAM them shut, when we should walk through them and stay awhile. In or out; indecisiveness about which door to walk through and stay, or which door to keep shut and never open, is easier to figure out with one thing in mind. As mom and dad use to say, don't let the door hit you in the ass on the way out. If you're not quite sure what that means, here's the short version: don't regret which doors you choose to open and which ones you decide to close.

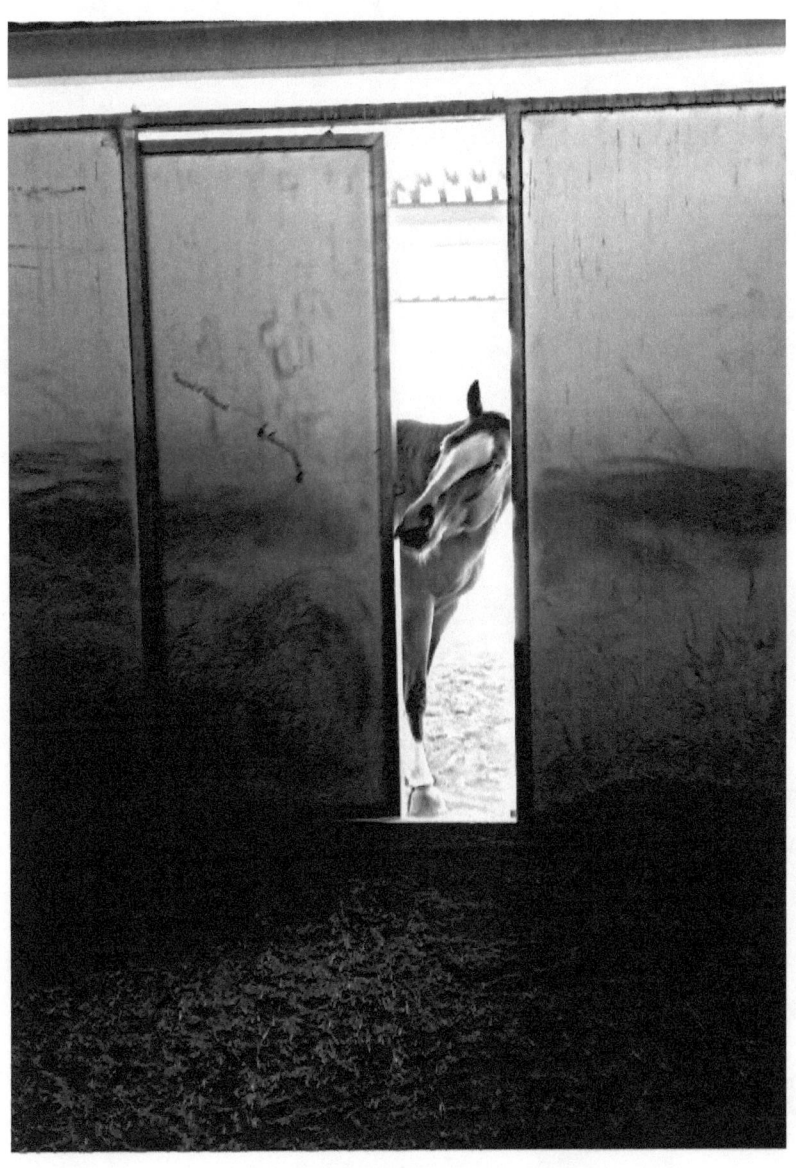

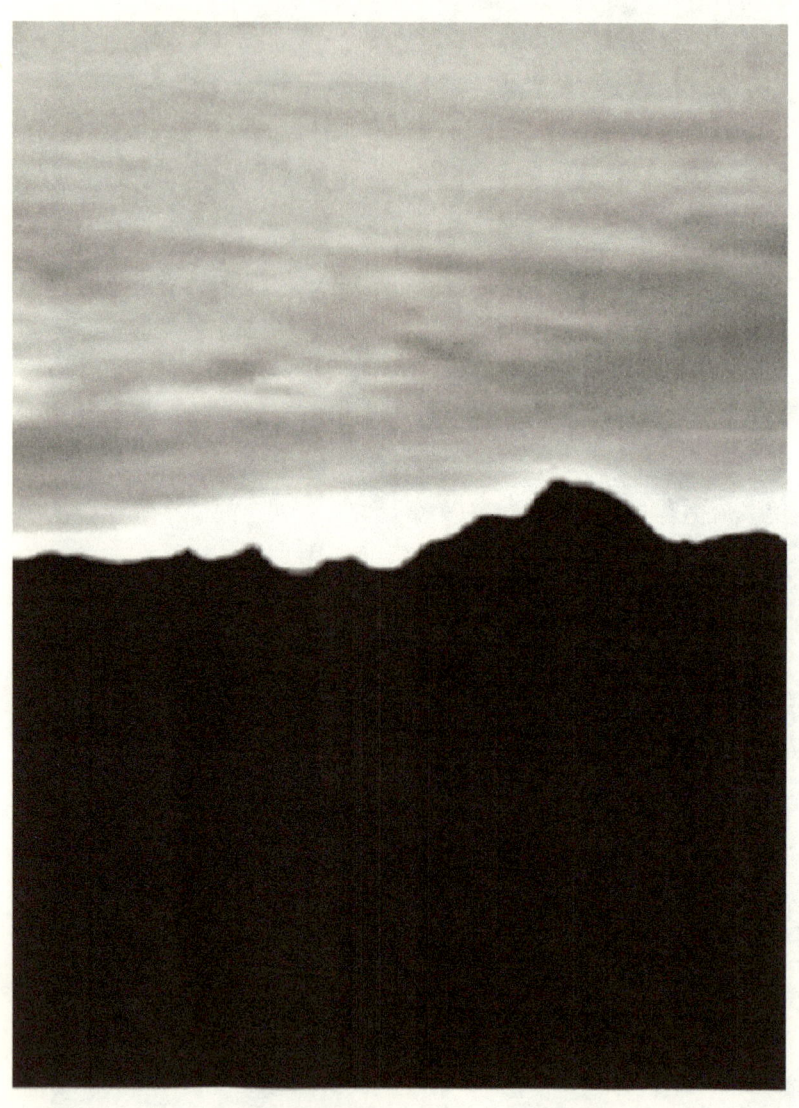

In The End

Evening rides with Jr are as unpredictable as Chicago weather in mid-September; some evenings it's a calm cool seventy degrees with clear skies; other times it a hail and wind storm without warning. For months I tried to figure out how to make every sunset ride with Jr pleasurable and not like a game of Russian Roulette. Through the process of elimination, the mystery was finally solved; Jr is addicted to dinner. Not just dinner but it must be served by a certain time every day or he goes from my pretty pony to the incredible hulk in 5.3 seconds. Amazing what a creature of habit he is. One evening on my way to the stables, I called my friend and suggested we try feeding before we ride just to see how Jr behaves and so we did. The ride that evening was so good I had to look down every so often just to be sure it was Jr I was riding. I knew he was food driven, but I had no idea to what extent the power of food controlled him. Sure, through rigorous training (intense human to horse arguing), I could break him of this addiction but why? He's not some young punk kid that needs to learn a lesson about life. He's a horse that has given many rides to many people over many years, and before his current dwelling place, he lived in a confined space with little contact to other life and where food was probably his only pleasure. Aside from some typical horse behaviors that need adjusting, he is a good natured beast. So adjusting my schedule to give him a little feed after a long day before a ride is a small price to pay for a happy horse. I have much bigger battles to fight with him that are a matter of importance; choosing my battles wisely makes life more pleasant for the both of us. It's all a matter of what matters most: what your goal is and what priority you place on the outcome you desire. Your methods and means to achieving your goal takes counting the cost of what you lose in retrospect to what you gain. When all is said and done, with all things considered, will what you have to sacrifice be worth what you acquire in the end?

It Just Is What It Is

Jr has become such a big part of my life that him being an animal I almost feel silly saying that. Though he is the first horse I've owned, he's not the first I've ridden. There is one horse out here in Arizona named Cimmeron that I have ridden many times, because the first time I rode him we instantly connected. Cimmeron is a very large horse that, from what the Wranglers have told me, doesn't really bond with his riders. Yet, the first time I rode him, Lee, the Wrangler leading our group, was amazed at the attentiveness Cimmeron showed me. Lee kept commenting on how Cimmeron would look back at me often, like he was checking on me and when I brushed this 1,600 pound beast, he became a gentle giant, just this big mushy lovable ball of fur. If Cimmeron would have been for sale, I would have done whatever necessary to buy him. Unfortunately, that was not an option; Cimmeron was not available to be mine and he never will be. His future is controlled by the trail ride owners, and being a good working horse, I am sure the benefits of having him around would make them crazy to let him go. It's disappointing, but I visited him often until my life and time became consumed with my own horse. Every chance I get to bring friends on a trail ride we go to Cimmeron's ranch and everyone there knows to have him ready for me. It amazes me that months can go by and this horse remembers me; if given the chance today, I'd pay whatever was asked to have this big boy be a part of my horse-loving world.

There are so many comparisons I could make with Cimmeron to life. Cimmeron, though alive and well, is an enjoyable part of my recent past, and I guess sometimes visiting the past isn't such a bad thing. But living in the now and preparing for the future prevents me from giving Cimmeron and me the pleasure of each other's company. Investing my time, heart and soul into him would be like investing into the bank of Clyde set up behind my local 7 Eleven; an investment that guarantees no return on that investment.

Cimmeron is also that thing I want so bad, but isn't an option to be had; he reminds me that no matter how perfect something may seem, no matter how convinced I am about its perfection, the world is a much bigger place than what surrounds me. Wanting what we cannot have, when by all indications it would be a good thing, has a way of challenging the deepest part of my logical thinking. As I think about Cimmeron, I am learning to accept this seemingly simple principle: that sometimes you need to accept what is or is not, try not to make sense of it and just let it go. If something you deeply desire is not an option for reasons out of your control, there is nothing you can do to make it otherwise.

I would love nothing more than to convince those who have control over Cimmeron to relinquish that control. There may be the chance he wouldn't want to come anyway, but unless he miraculously become Mr. Ed and could speak up for himself, I will never know. For now, it just is what it is.

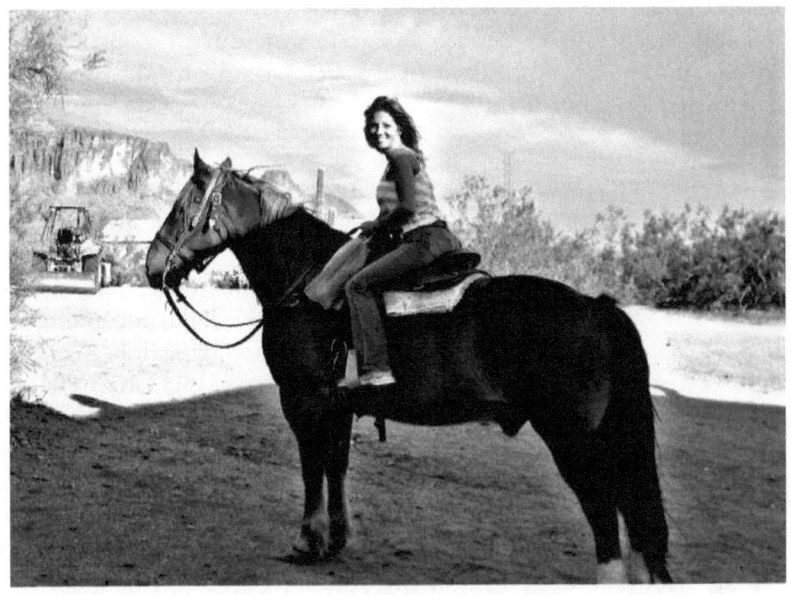

Let's Play

One of the things I do with Jr before we set off on a ride is bring him in the arena and run him; I don't ride him but use a whip (not to whip him) to have him just run in circles and work out any issues he has or extra energy needing to be expelled before I get on him and ride. This time in the arena also sets his mind right about who is in charge. He will inevitably challenge me and try to run the other way or just stop when he feels like it. The sound of the whip is enough to get him back on track and reminds him that I'm calling the shots. One night he ran a little, challenged me a little and simply just didn't feel like doing the whole thing. I could appreciate his lack of motivation as I too was uninspired, so without a lead he followed me around the arena a few times paying full attention to me. We just kept walking. Then I picked up the pace and we started running; we had so much fun! He just wanted to play while he exercised, and he wanted to do it by my side. I am sure this would have been frowned on since I put the whip down, but it was a moment we both needed.

I am perceived as a go getter, independent thinker and strong woman who can handle anything…alone. Just like Jr though, there are times when having someone by your side to share in the moment makes it easier to accomplish your task. Never underestimate the value of those you trust that want to walk beside you. Don't take them for granted and be very careful of carrying the world on your shoulders alone. As I have learned, you very well may be able to do it alone, but why? There are millions of people within your reach. Hold on to the few you can trust that want to keep up with your pace, be it fast or slow and they will ease your soul when the world crashed down on your shoulders. Life is meant to be shared, enjoyed and lived. The "things" we acquire are just that, things. People and what they give you is an indelible part of your life that no "thing" can take the place of. My stubborn, Ms. Independent self is learning to let those who want to walk beside me do so. If nothing else, it will make for an interesting life.

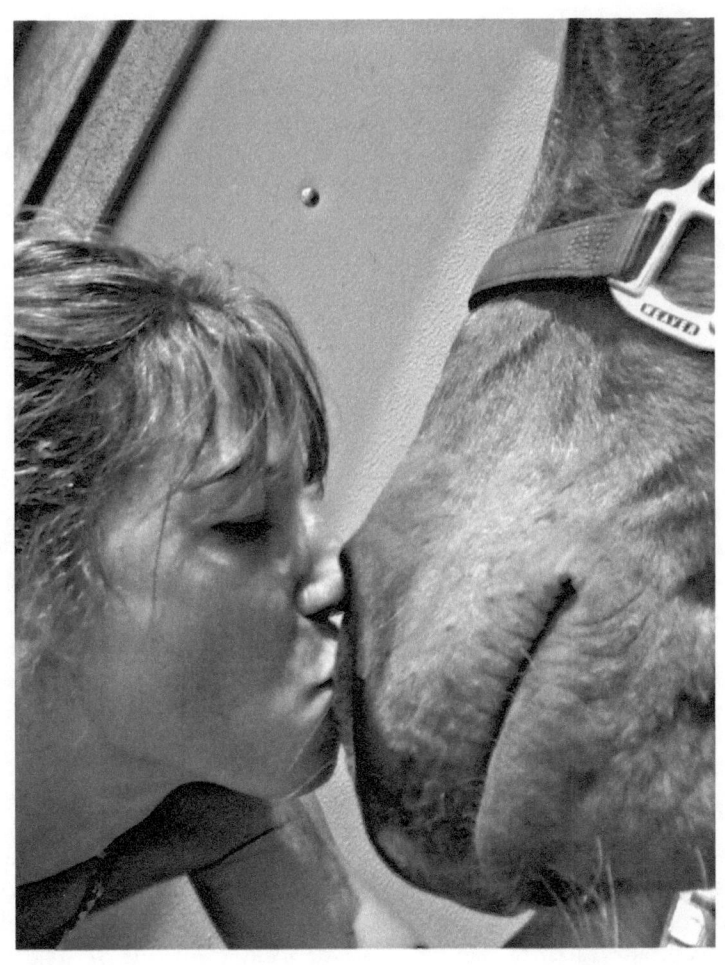

Mare, Mare in the Stall

Cali and Filly are the mares ("may er" female horse) of the Terri Ranch Inn. Cali, a white paint horse with a horse racing history, is as beautiful as any horse you've seen in the movies. She is tall, thick, and has clearly established among the boys that she is the boss. Jr is the elder horse and as far as the pecking order, the other horses respect that, but Cali pretty much rules the roost. Cali's hang up, as I've learned, is she does not like you touching her ears.

Filly is a Blue Roan, a Quarter Horse who is greyish, almost blue, hence the name. She came to the ranch recently and as a former barrel racer, she is spunky! One day while trail riding, I watched in awe as Terri came flying down the trail on her. Terri, who was probably born on a horse, couldn't believe how fast Filly was. That really is saying a lot about spunky, speedy Filly.

The way the stalls are set up with two next to each other, it was made very clear not to allow the mares next to each other. The girls would fight, and it wouldn't be pretty. Mares tend to compete for dominance. I have to chuckle when I think about this; having four older sisters, I've see a lot of battles ensue over who's in charge. Not much unlike my sisters, I have found, with the mares, that they have their own personalities. I approach them differently; they respond differently. As long as their differences are acknowledged, everyone is happy.

Being the "baby" of five girls, though different for all of us, maintained a common thread; we all wanted to be our own person. The pecking order was clearly defined by age. Being the youngest, there was a long way to go before I even got my own room! I was the guinea pig who had her eyebrows plucked off (still haven't completely grown back), legs shaved too young, twelve inches of hair cut off, ash blonde coloring turned red, always wore hand me downs (that went out of style by the time I got them), and couldn't go to school, CCD, church, the store, anywhere without hearing "Do you have a sister named Pam, Karla, Dora, or Sue?" Talk about identity crises and self-esteem issues! Every time I'd looked in the mirror, I'd wondered who the heck I was because I certainly didn't have my own identity. But on the flip side, I also got to go to concerts on Harleys before I hit high school, be a co-pilot in a drag race, be tossed around as high as the roof flipping around backward, go dancing in the local bars at 16 and hang out with the cool high school kids while in Junior High, and I knew if I ever needed anything four of my best friends would be there for me. They would listen to me complain, dry my tears, make me laugh until I pee my pants, and love me even when I felt unlovable. Sisters, they love you like mothers, beat you up like brothers, protect you like fathers and stick with you like best friends.

Cali and Filly worked it out, just as my sisters and I have always worked it out. Now when I look in the mirror I know exactly who I am... I little bit of Pam, a little bit of Karla, a little bit of Dora, a little bit of Sue, and a whole lot of just me. Mirror, mirror on the wall, who's the fairest of them all? That's just fairy tale jibberish...we are all perfectly ourselves; I am just the lucky one to have the best part of each of my sisters stick with me to shape me into who I am today.

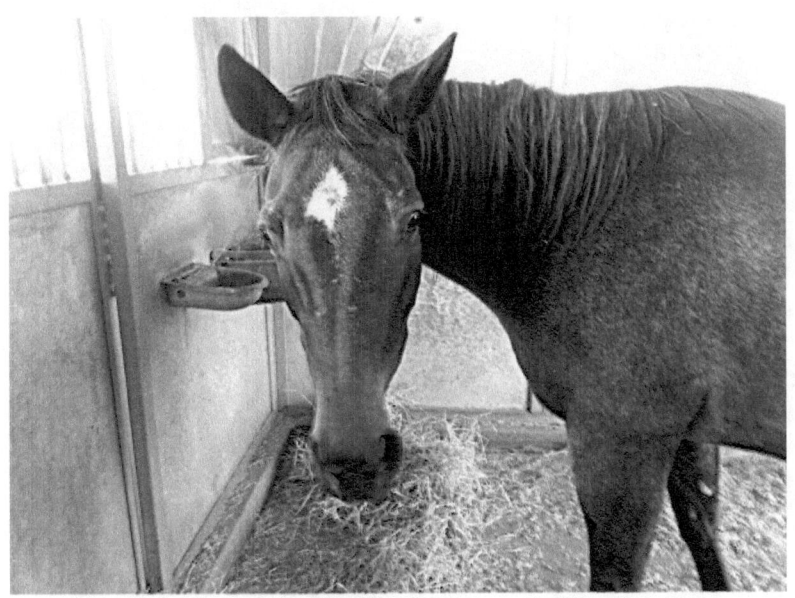

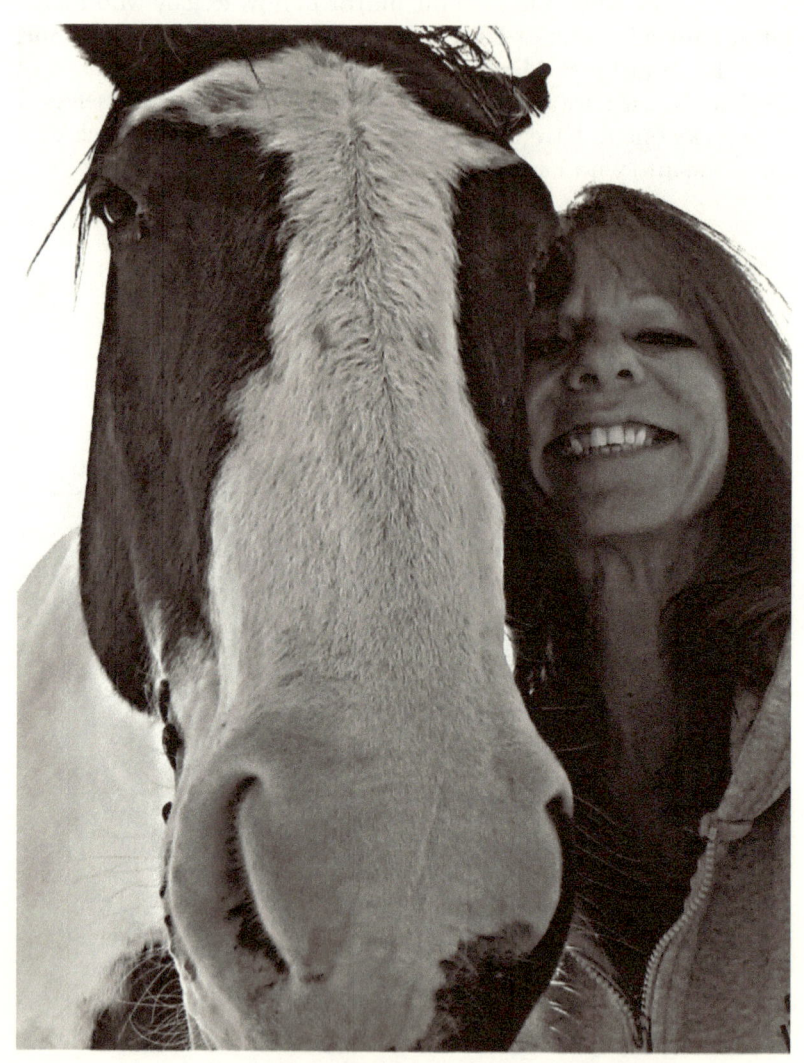

Musical Buckets

One of the most peculiar things about horses is their eating habits. Jr's horse family consist of three other horses and one additional buddy that boards with him. They all have their own "room" (stall) with shade, a feeding bin and water bucket. Stalls are typical in size with an area outside to move around a bit. Though these rooms are nice for a horse, they are not nearly enough space for a horse to get adequate exercise if left there every day. During the hot summer, two or three horses are put in the arena (a large enclosed area) to run free around dinner time when the heat of the day has passed. Feeding in the arena is in some ways easier, in others rather interesting. It's easier for obvious reason; you can feed three at once! The interesting part comes if you don't put the feed in the arena before the horses. Hay in your possession when entering the arena makes you like a rat dropped in a box of cats. Thankfully our babies (horses) are well mannered and for the most part, they all just rush you, stop and stick close to your side until you drop the hay in their feed bins. In the evening the horses get a special meal, a mix of pellets and the "good stuff" (multi nutrient pellets) that obviously taste quite yummy. After the hay is set and the horses are eating, you come in with buckets (Jr's is purple) and dump them on top of the hay. Of course, they hear the pellets as you scoop them in the buckets and watch you walk towards them. All the horses attentively follow your every step as they wait for you to step into the arena and like little kids anticipating a piece of candy, cannot wait to have at 'em. What's most peculiar is though they are all the same pellets and equal amounts are put in each bucket, what the other horse has is always better. These three large animals begin playing "musical buckets." Round and round they go. Bucket number one Jr, number two Cali, number three Leroy, for about twenty seconds before Jr moves to Leroy's bucket while Cali takes Jr's and Leroy looks, finds Cali's and quickly moves in to resume consumption. Twenty seconds later round and round they go again. Occasionally there's a little argument among them as they play this game, and it's so silly because, my goodness, they all have the same thing in their bucket!!!!

This reminds me of dinner time in the neighborhood. Mom and the neighbor's mom could be making the exact same thing for dinner; actually, mom could even make it and secretly send it to the neighbors, yet it just tastes so much better next door! Mom could even be a better cook (she is) than the neighbor and still, we would prefer to eat the spam surprise that Dana's having just because Dana is having it. I always thought it was just "human nature" to want what others have; obviously horses have adopted the same behavior.

I find humor in the arena feeding time rituals among Jr and the gang and always try to explain to Jr that he has the same thing, but it does no good; round and round they go. They burn more calories getting to their food than they actually consume when they reach the bottom of the food bin. Almost makes eating senseless. Funny, when we find ourselves pursuing what others have we senselessly waste a lot of time, brain cell activity and energy thinking we can have something better when all we need and more has freely been given to us. Perhaps if we spent more time being grateful for what we have and not looking so intently at what others have, we would find ourselves content, at peace and richly blessed.

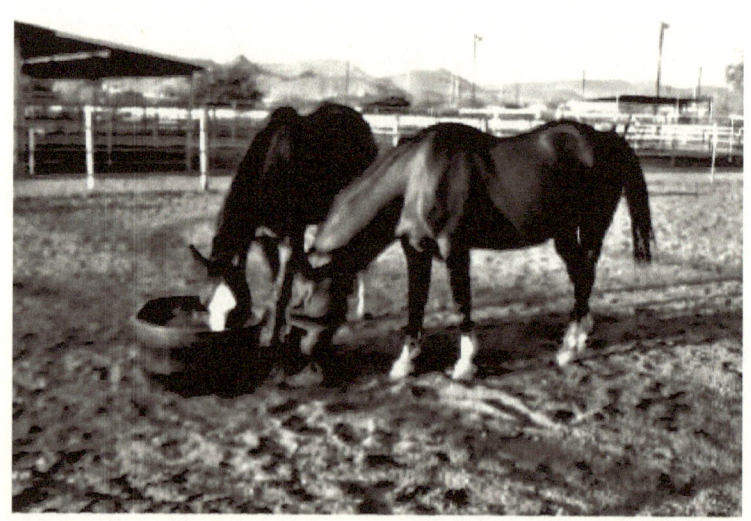

No Shit

One of the less fun tasks of horse ownership is cleaning stalls. Don't get me wrong; I don't mind it. It is actually therapeutic in a way. However, I must say there is always the inevitable moment I know is coming every time I finish cleaning up everyone's stall, the arena and yard, and put the bucket and shovel away...Jr decides it's a great time to lift his tail, let breakfast find its way to the just cleaned stall, and leave me a nice big pile. Why oh why must he wait until I am finished? Of course, after an hour or more of shoveling to make sure I got every little bit, I simply cannot just leave it there; it would drive me crazy. Cleaning the living quarters of animals is important for health reasons; so it must be done. Standing, walking and lying around in their own waste can cause infections, parasites, weaken/damage their hoofs, cause thrush etc... It certainly makes sense, after all, it's waste, the icky stuff, the part of what is ingested that has no benefit to the health of a physical being. We all know this, yet metaphorically speaking, why do we allow ourselves to live in unclean stalls? We walk in it, stand in it, sleep in it and wonder why on earth we are sick? Crazy as it sounds, there is a simple parallel in this example; when you smell it, see it, feel it, just pick up the bucket and shovel and remove it. It can be a tiring task. You can feel like you just finished cleaning up one mess, but inevitably you will encounter yet another that needs to be removed. You can let it sit there for another time, but I don't really need to expound on what happens after horse poop sits a few days. I know it sounds simple; the reality is, it is. There is just no artistic, secret, masterful way to shovel shit.

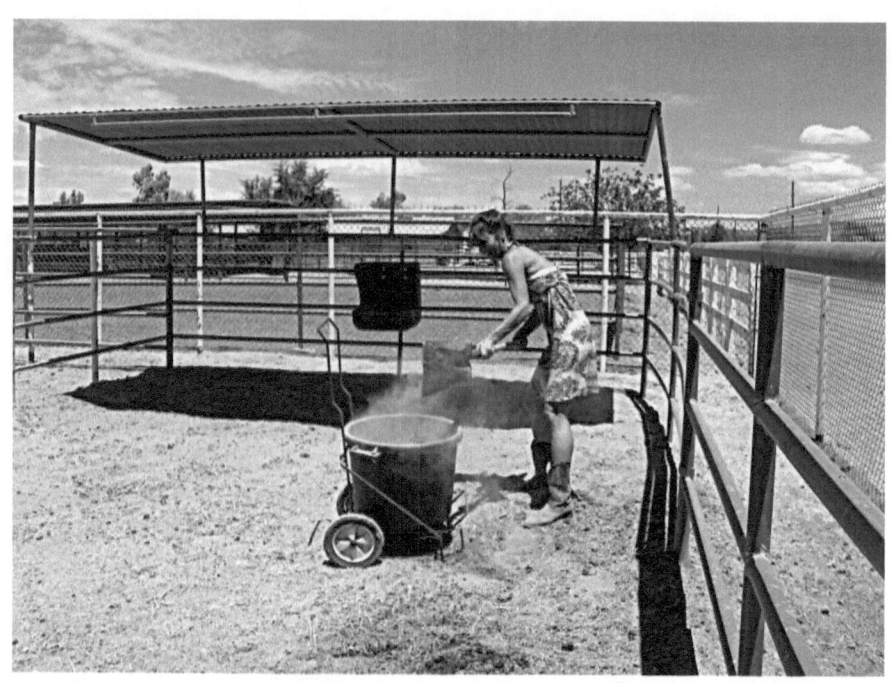

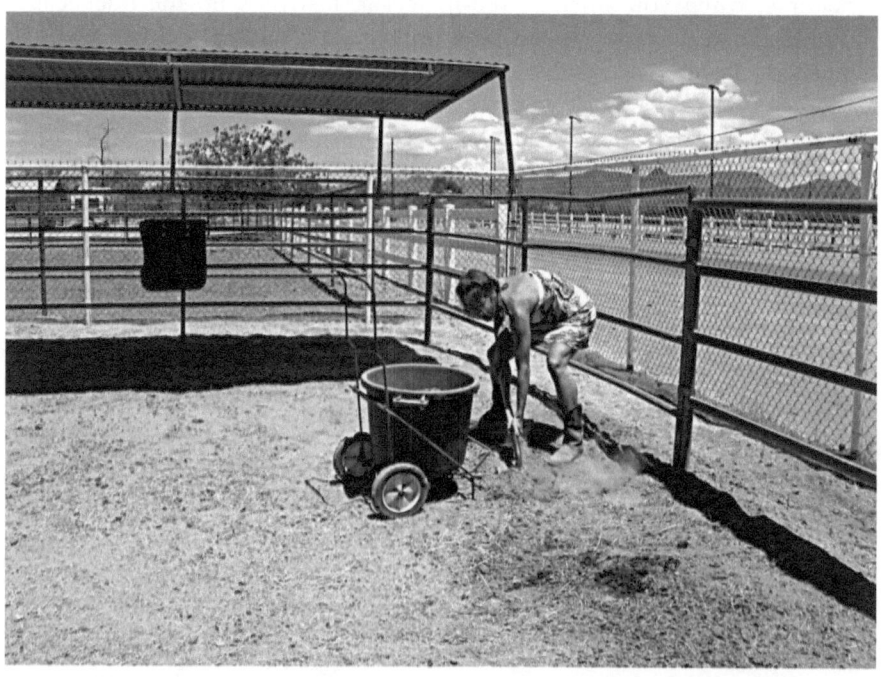

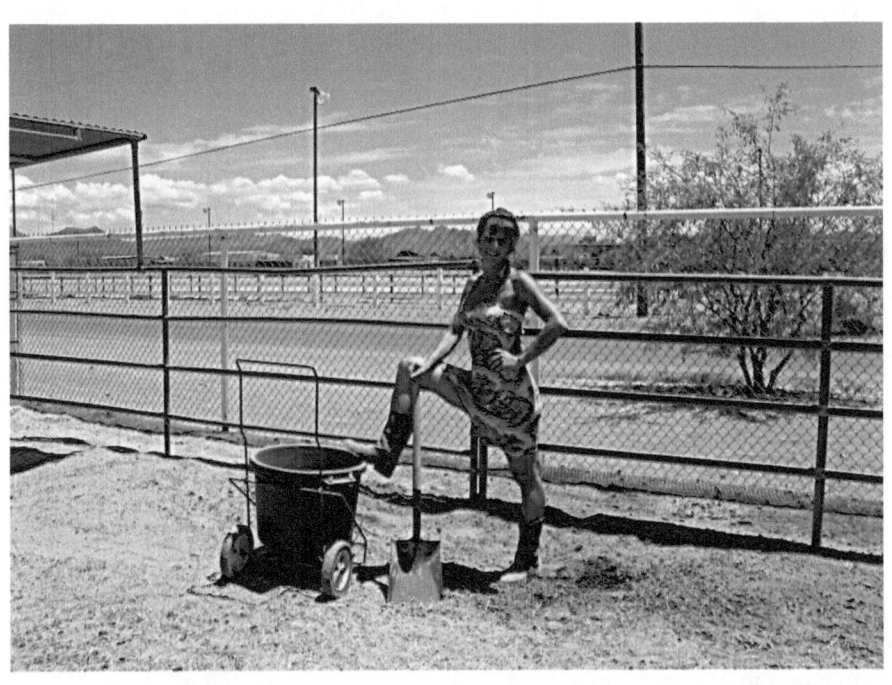

Oh So Spooky

Horses are very large animals; they are strong, powerful, large living breathing beings. When my friend and I head out on a ride, we joke about the imaginary demons that spook our horses when we ride the same path we've taken what seems like 113 times. "Oh, NO! What's that…oh my God!!!!…. It's a large rock on the path… Run!!!" Seriously, neither of us can see what the problem is when our horse does a quick stop and takes a few steps back or to the side. We look around, and we just don't see any reason for their fear. We make light of it because our minds cannot grasp how such a large animal with a brain can be so intimidated and afraid of what we see as non-threatening and something they've seen before. There are so many reasons: pent up energy from a lack of exercise and type of diet, barn sour, even certain pain they may have. The biggest reason I've heard is horses are prey animals, and everything they see is a potential predator. When something spooks them, they immediately just become survivalists. As I watched Jr during a spooking session, he tends to slightly hop and stop, maybe take one or two steps sideways. I notice when I touch him and talk him through it, telling him it's ok and divert his attention, we get through those spooky moments relatively quick. I've learned that when I broaden the scope of my view and try to see as he sees, as prey, there can be some pretty scary things out there. Jr is a very smart horse, his registered name is "Centella Bueno" (meaning good genius), and he lives up to. When he steps back, I can almost feel him assessing and processing the situation. He lets me distract him, but really, when it comes to survival, he needs to remain in control of himself no matter how much he trusts me.

Life can be spooky for all of us. Fear of the unknown, fear of failure, etc… Fear, for each of us, is motivated by different means. Every one of us fears something, and chances are no one else can see or grasp why on earth we would fear that. When I sit up on Jr and we encounter spooky moments, I've learned to let him assess and process the situation. I have learned that, though it is necessary to have that moment, if I allow him to be immobile too long, it feeds his fear, and he then wants to run back to home, despite his hoof pounding attitude to get out when we are there. I am really not much different than Jr; sometimes the misery of what I know can be easier to live with than facing the fear of what I do not know. Comparable to horse spooks, when I face fear, I allow myself a minute to assess and process if my fear is even rational. In any case, it is vital for me to move past the initial moment of heart-stopping, second-guessing, everything around you is closing in moment one step at a time.

I've come to realize my fear is controlled by me alone; if I truly want to grow and experience life, I have to accept that fear is inevitable. I can either confront it or….well, if I want to live while I'm alive, there really is no other option.

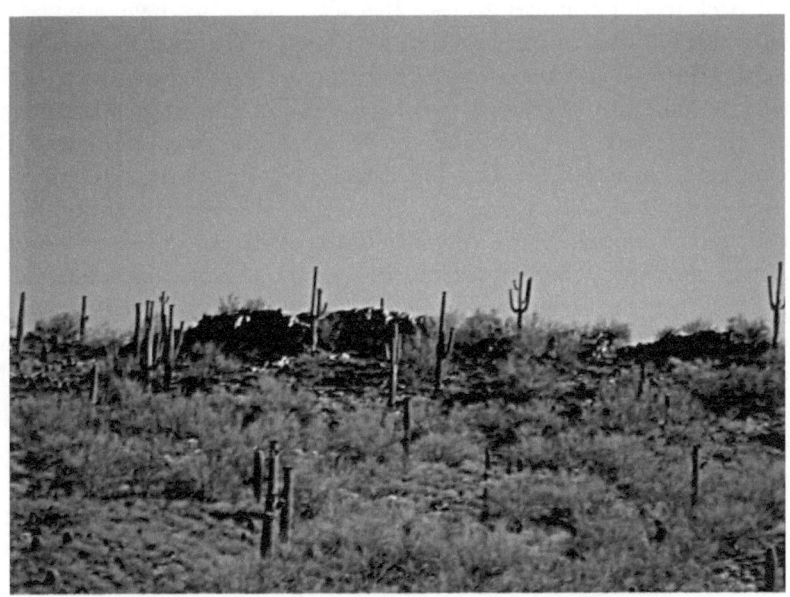

Repetition, Repetition, Repetition

Horses are not much unlike humans when it comes to habits. Jr never ceases to amaze me that after what seems like a million times of repeating the same desired action for my desired reaction, if we don't do it for a while, he reverts back to his comfort zone of undesirable behavior. Thankfully, each time we find ourselves starting over, it take a lot less time for him to remember what it is he should do.

Isn't that the truth about us silly humans? No matter what opportunities we may have for a better way of living, we find it easier to revert back to our comfort zones. Just like horses, we have a will; what differs with us is we're not as smart as a horse. We tend to fight within ourselves through justifying our misery for the sake of comfort. Jr has fought me on many occasions, but I have found that when I confidently stand my ground, he inevitably gives in. Little does he know that sometimes I have no idea why I'm doing what I'm doing. He trusts me because, despite myself, I trust myself. Trust of oneself is an interesting feat in life. I suppose if we did that more often our comfort would be found in knowing, whether we can be certain or not, that what we are doing may not be easier, but is better for us. Is it really that simple? Nothing is ever that simple, but I have learned when I start with me and trust myself, there is nothing that can come against me and prevail. My inner peace is strong enough to sustain me through to the next new habitual way of living for even a better life.

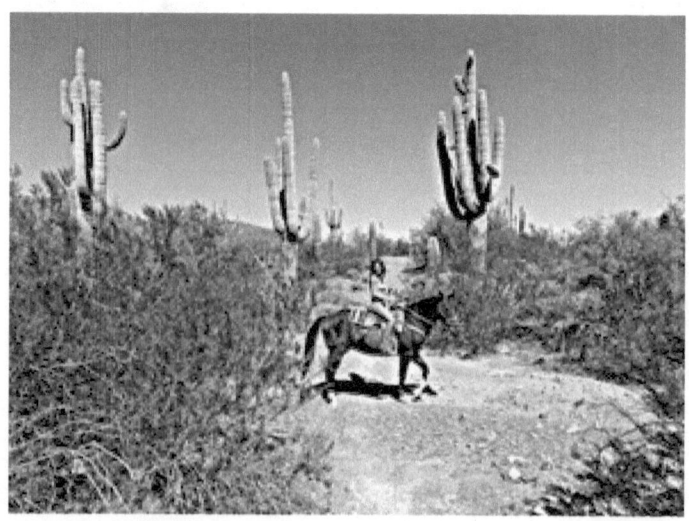

The Moments In Between

One of the most valuable moments with my horse is grooming him. I can spend hours just brushing, petting and hugging him. Though I know he is no Mr. Ed, I tell him everything and he communicates with me very clearly. When he picks his head up and wraps it around my neck, he's hugging me, when he rubs his long nose up and down my back he's telling me he's happy, when he lifts his upper lip when I kiss his muzzle, he's telling me he loves me too. Of course, when he pounds his right hoof into the ground repeatedly, he is making sure I know he doesn't like me giving the other horses any attention; this is our time. When I am happy, sad, angry, or anxious, I always look him in the eye and without any body movement, his eyes tell me if he is engaged in the moment or if his mind is elsewhere, like on meal time. Communicating with your horse this way is important; it creates a bond that builds mutual trust between horse and rider. Too often in life we overlook the necessary moments in time that give trust substance. It's not in the words, the actions, or the busyness of that moment. It's the investment of time that shows there is no other place you'd rather be; it is found between the breaths you breathe, the stillness between movements and the essence that surrounds the moment. These things in life cannot be created or made to be, they are the uncontrollable elements of what makes for being at peace with your world. Slow down, take heed to the moment and realize what is most important in life isn't created by the moments you try to make but the moments in between

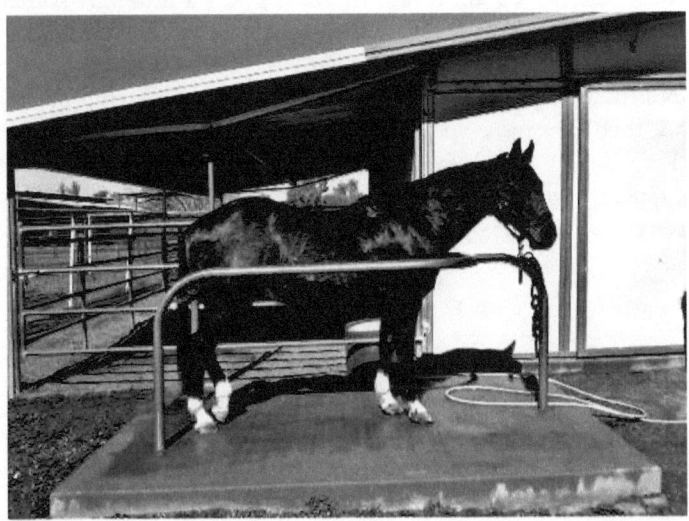

Rollin, Rollin, Rollin....

It's the most peculiar thing to me that after spending the better part of an hour washing my horse, brushing him and another hour letting him dry, that he finds it impossible not to roll in the dirt! I really enjoyed the first bath I gave Jr; he seemed to enjoy it. I didn't really know I should let him dry completely before letting him loose, and he was acting a little agitated when I finished his bath. Here I was thinking, like a new horse owner, maybe the shampoo is irritating him or something that, of course, wasn't simple animal behavior. Not being sure what his problem was, I rinsed him off again. Sure enough, that wasn't it; he became more agitated! With this, I took him to the arena to let walk him a bit and see how he behaved just to be sure nothing was wrong with him. What do you think he did? Immediately, he rolled...first to the right, then to the left...then the big shaking off of what dirt didn't compact into a thick layer of mud on his body. Oh, that wasn't all, as I watch in utter amazement that he would do that after all that grooming time, he walks up to me and rubs his body all over me! He was so happy. After researching this animal behavior, I have come to learn that horses roll for a lot of reason, and it is actually very healthy for them. They roll for pleasure, self-grooming (really?), relieve pain or discomfort, and for rest. The way a horse rolls is actually an indicator of its health, and based on this research, Jr is very healthy.

Sometimes I find myself rolling knee deep in sloppy mud and wonder what the heck I am doing there. I guess a little dirt sometimes is healthy, and my reasons for being there irrelevant. The key is to get back off the ground, shake of the dust and let what sticks do what it's supposed to whatever that may be. Now if you find pleasure staying in the messy, dirty mud, then you have an entirely different problem; you can only roll in it so long before you become dirt yourself. Horses roll, but they get back up, quickly, with energy; it's as if that rollin' around is medicinal and gives them renewed strength to take on the next adventure.

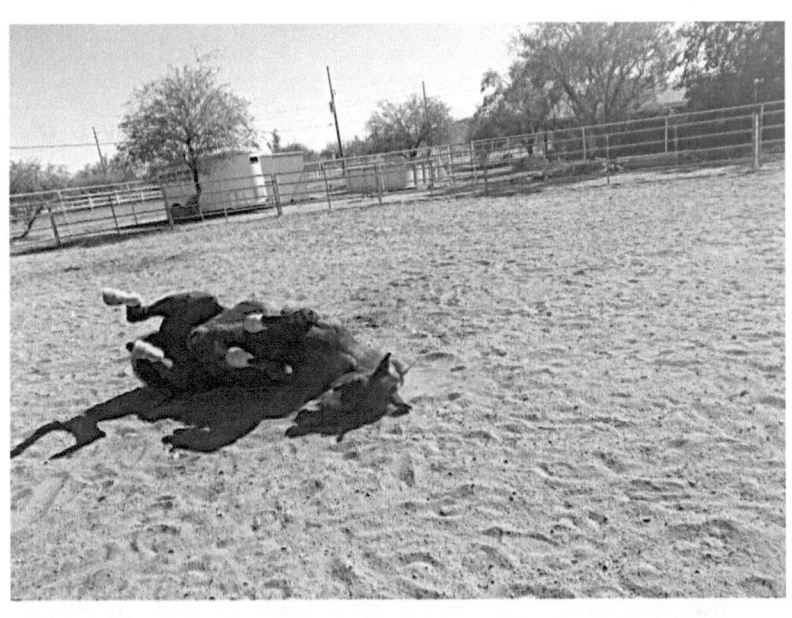

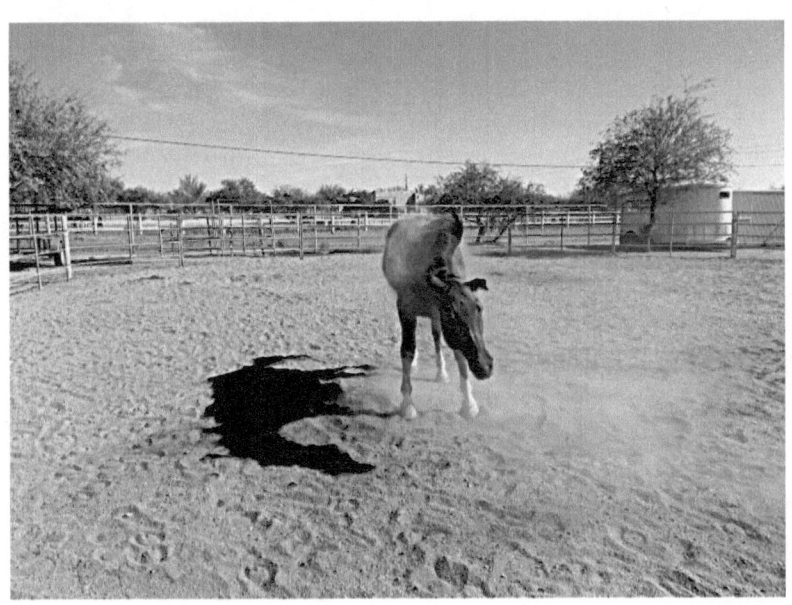

Shoo Fly!

Since relocating to Arizona, I was under the misconception that they don't really have a lot of flies out here, until recently. The reason I thought that was because at work and at home, I truly have only seen maybe five flies in three years. It all makes perfect sense to me now why that is; all the flies in Arizona are hovering in swarms irritating and agitating my horse! The heat of summer has brought these pesky, annoying, six legged, two winged bugs out to feed on my beautiful, white socked, bay (brownish), black mane and tailed baby. Being the pampering horse mama I am; I, of course, apply fly spray frequently. Jr handles the fly ordeal just fine. Aside from the occasional tail swat and protection of a fly mask, he's pretty much unaffected by these miniature monsters. I cannot even fathom it; when I am with him and he is infested, they irritate the heck out of me! Certainly, at minimum, it has to slightly annoy him. Yet you would never know it.

When driving to work every day, I encounter an infestation of flies in my own world; this would be Arizona drivers attempting the daunting feat of merging into and out of traffic. Every single weekday morning I encounter the same issues and yell with all out road rage, "MERGE ASSHOLE!" Then I sigh, shake my head and try to release the tension in my neck and shoulders. How is it an animal can control his ability to not go absolutely nuts on hundreds of tiny little biting bugs all over his body, yet I cannot control my anger with strangers who are in cars, sharing the road and not really affecting my existence other than inconveniencing how fast I can drive my car? Too bad they don't make merge spray! Since they don't, I am learning to relax a little more behind the wheel, see it for what it is (despite the stupidity of other drivers) and share the road. It's just amazing to me how a little perspective can challenge your behavior patterns. Though I'd like to live in my own little world, I don't and I must share it. If I must share it, I guess its best I take my cues from Jr on how to not let the little fly-sized things be earth shattering.

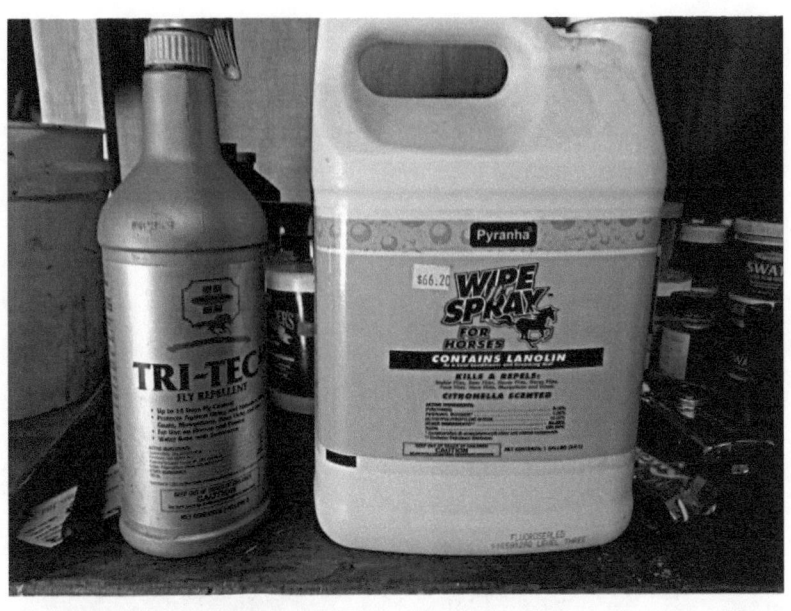

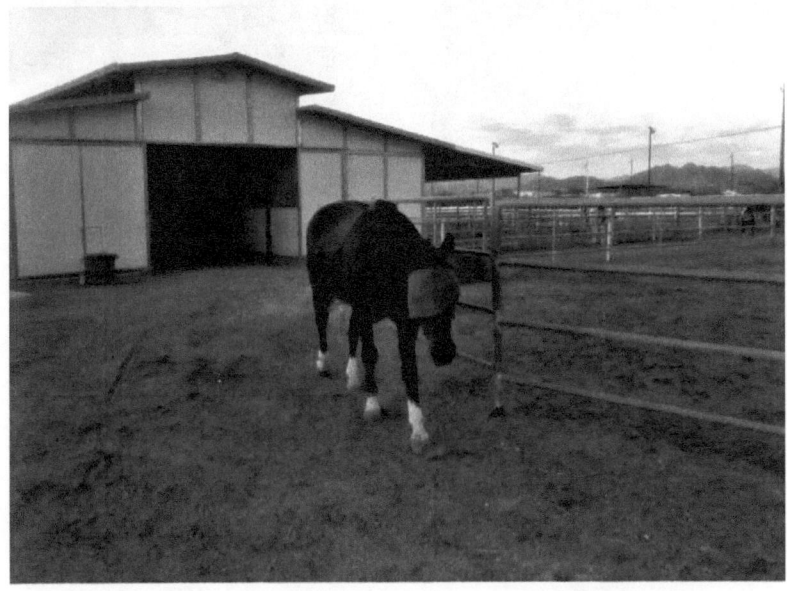

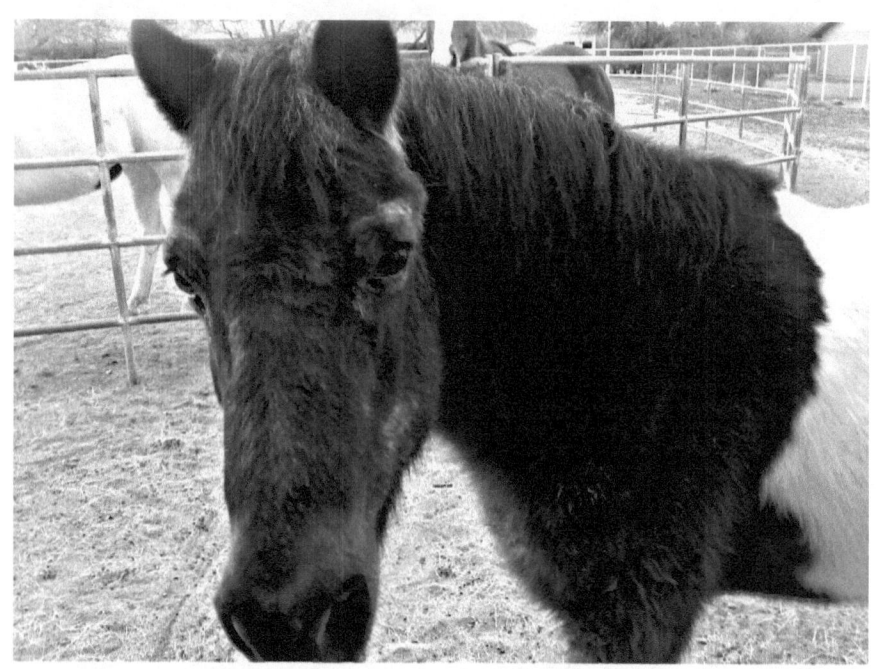

Stand Back Buddy

It was almost a year before I knew Boomer's name. Boomer, or "Pony" as we call him, is another boarded animal in the gang. Boomer is a good boy who gave pony rides for many years. He's not mean on any level. He's not even cranky, though you would think so by the way he avoids human contact. He is simply beautiful when just bathed and brushed. For whatever reason though, Boomer seems almost afraid to allow humans close; well, except for kids. He seems most at ease with little girls. He handles us bigger humans just fine when he has to. He actually even seems to enjoy being brushed and loved. It's just getting past the initial point of contact.

I've learned a lot about myself interacting with Pony. Even though he is a pony, don't be fooled; their hoofs can hit you just as hard as a large horse. So there is no misconception about his ability to do bodily harm. He may give you a "stand back buddy don't mess with me" look that can be intimidating, but really he's a good boy who enjoys being coddled. I can relate to his hesitancy with humans. He comes off afraid yet has the power to protect himself. He tends to approach his uncertainty by being proactive as oppose to protective by choice-less circumstances. The problem with this is, had I not taken a gentle approach with him and invested time into understanding how to reach him, I never would have come to love this stand-back buddy named Boomer; he would have just been "Pony" without a name who stayed in his own little world. Kind of makes me check myself when I withdraw into my own little world and give those who try to get close a "stand back buddy" look. Not all people are bad; some have the best of intentions and can even make a difference in my life if I let them. Seeing my "stand back buddy" self from the other view gives me a whole new perspective; so glad Boomer wasn't just a nameless pony. He's so close he's family now, and I couldn't imagine the gang without him.

The 5 P's

Learning is mostly done by doing for me, but I did learn a lesson from simply observing another rider. Interestingly, he was not a novice. I actually admire his confidence and control with the horses. He had five horses running circles in the area without the use of a whip. I was amazed. He offers typically good advice and is very patient in his approach with humans. However, this same person experienced a perfectly preventable situation with his horse. While returning from a ride, we noticed his horse lost a shoe! It just fell off. This is not the norm. He dismounted and started walking him back, reigns in his pocket just casually walking. Within minutes, one of the reigns slipped out, his horse stepped on it, got spooked and sure enough, broke his bit. Poor Snickers (his horse) just wasn't having a good day.

The unfortunate thing in this experience is that had Snickers' shoes been maintained it never would have fallen off, and if his owner had been more attentive and held on to the reigns, the bit wouldn't have broken. This could not have been a comfortable thing for Snickers, a piece of metal ripping out of his mouth, through his teeth. What did I learn? Well first, that I can learn a whole lot just by watching, but it also reinforced the idea of not cutting corners. In life and in riding, maintenance and attentiveness, even with the mundane, really sets us up for success or failure. Some things we just may not feel like doing because we've done it a million times before, but the effects of neglect have a way of causing unnecessary harm. As a friend of mine use to tell me often "Always remember the Five P's...Proper Preparation Prevents Poor Performance."

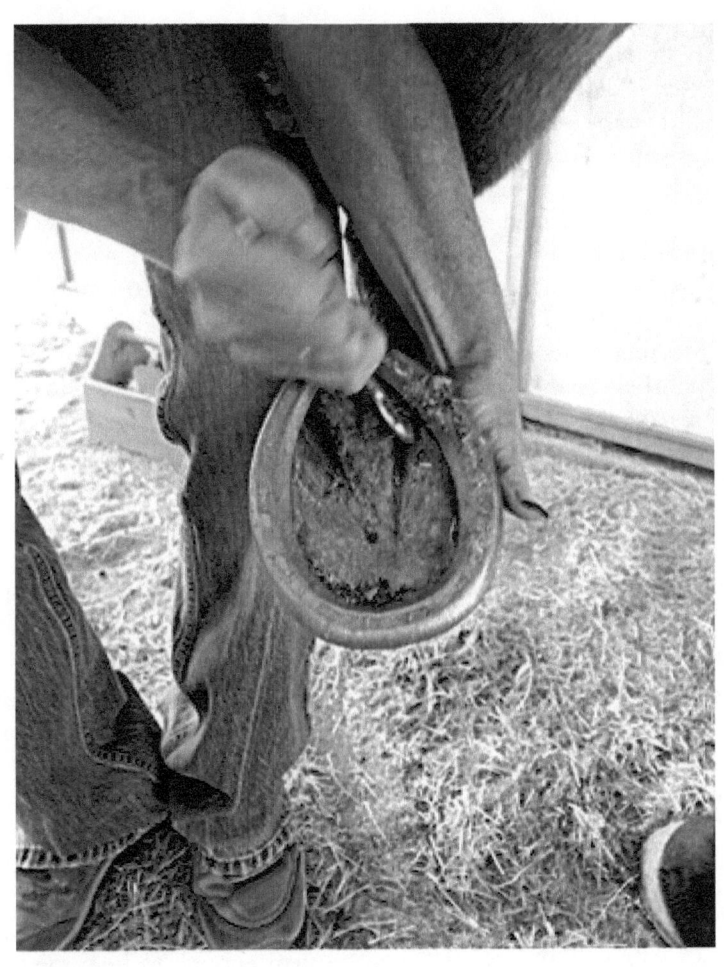

To Be Like My Horse

Jr and I have a unique bond. Of course, those who love horses, dogs, or even cats can understand that unique pet to owner relationship. I have chuckled at the saying that "some of my best friends have never said a word to me" because as funny as that sounds it is profoundly true. Jr's warm welcome, excited to see me pursuit when I arrive, his head hugging, muzzle rubbing up against me when I am sad, his walks beside me when he knows I just need to unload the thoughts in my mind or sorrows in my heart and the way we dance when we are perfectly in sync is missed when we are miles apart. I know he'll be waiting for me to return, yet there are moments when I just feel like hanging out with him without distractions or pressing matters to rush my time with him, just "us" time. I know it's an unusual thing to say about an animal, but unfortunately, most people, no matter how wonderful they are, don't take the time to be that type of friend. Life has a way of keeping us busy, consumed with ourselves and distracted from those things that we say matter most. I suppose that's just normal, just life, just being human.

The words "that's just" in relation to these things should challenge us; as should statements that begin with words like "because I" as they tend to proceed excuses and justifications. Yes, I say them and when I step back and think about them, I challenge myself on whether I am making excuses or justifying something I want or don't want to do. When I think about that unique bond with Jr and challenge myself with the relationships that mean the most to me, I really have to stop and wonder if I am showing just what they really do mean to me. It's mind boggling how a horse can be the kind of friend I want to be to those I deeply love. I do so much for him because I love that hairy beast while knowing he's an animal and can do nothing tangible in return for me. It is a blessing when in return his attention and affections are what he does give, willingly. This has been more than enough to help me get through some pretty rough moments. With that said, how much more of a blessing is it for the people we love when we treat them with this level of consideration? Extending your investment of time, attention and affections with the knowledge of no tangible payback from them, shows them they matter and you care. This can impact their lives in ways that no money or thing could replace or compare in value. Simple enough and financially free, yet too often we let those moments slip by.

Uninspired

Not unlike any other aspect of life, sometimes the rigors of riding can challenge my inspiration. Some days I just want to get on my horse and ride without any issues, challenges, or excitement. I have learned this is not probable even on a good day. Jr, though a fairly mild natured horse, is still just that, a horse. He surprises me often with how in tune he can be to my moods; horses have been said to have a "sixth sense." Even if that were true, he still is incapable of simply just being and doing what I want, when I want and how I want all the time, no matter what my mood. Sure, I can continue to train him until he masters certain skills, but the reality is, every time you get on a horse, you have to have your mind fully engaged in what you are doing. The seemingly smallest thing can trigger major responses that can be disastrous. Thinking ahead and having a plan to keep you and your horse safe is vital to preventing dangerous situations. As in life, we must always be engaged mentally when we participate, have a plan so we can get to where we want to go and even when uninspired, maintain forward motion...even if it's just baby steps...unless of course living an uninspired life is your goal.

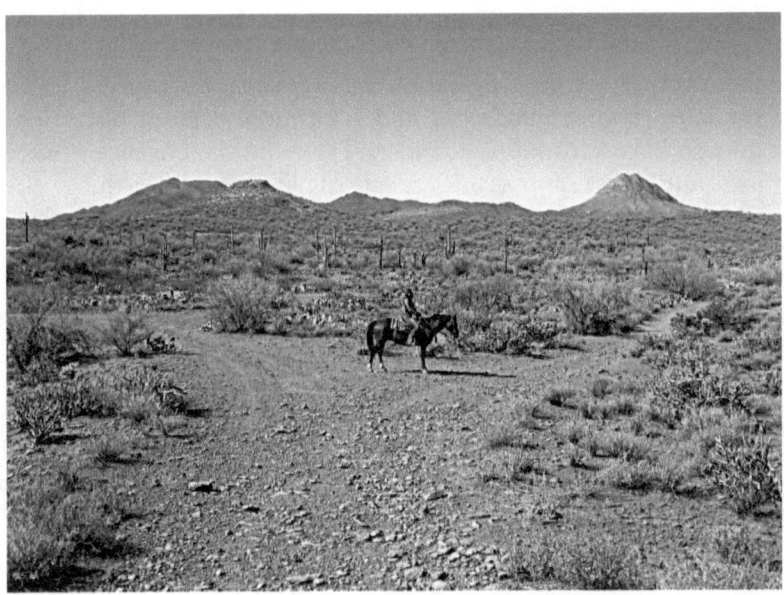

Until We Meet Again

As I sat on the plane flying away from Jr for the next two weeks, I was reminiscing about the trips I've taken, and the way he would seem so happy to see me when I returned. This was a longer trip than normal so I began to wonder if a horse has the concept of time and after so many days pass without me there, if he just kind of forgets me, but then remembers me when he sees me (out of sight out of mind). Odd thought I know, he's a horse for God's sake. I guess his reaction when I get to the ranch, before I even make my way to the stalls, has me convinced he is happy to see me. When my car pulls up and I get out of the car way across the arena from his stall, I see him head over to the fence just looking at me. As soon as I walk back, he waits to see if I am coming to the fence or the stall door, and he moves quickly to get to me every time. What a wonderful feeling that is, like he really did miss me.

This seemingly of little importance scenario reminds me of one thing that sticks out above all other things I learned from mom and dad; it was the way they would say goodbye to each other. I still clearly remember dad kissing mom and saying I love you every time he left. I have carried this with me since I can remember; it taught me from a very young age to never take for granted the time you have with people. When you part ways with someone, even for a short time, don't always be so sure that you will see them again. When you have this concept engraved into the back of your mind, you find a lot more value is placed on the time you do have with those you love. Time and the quality of that time becomes the most important aspect of life and everything else is secondary. This thinking has also created in me the appreciation that it is a blessing to see someone again and not to just brush off that meeting with a casual "it's just another moment with whoever again" attitude. Jr, though just a horse, with his eager head-bobbing, tail-wagging, quick steps to the stall door for a welcome home just makes me smile from the inside out. Of how much more value is it when we show those we love that they are worth our time, attention and effort? Time is money they say. I may not have a lot of either, but I do know my time, though limited, is rich with love and appreciation for those I am blessed to have had and have in my life.

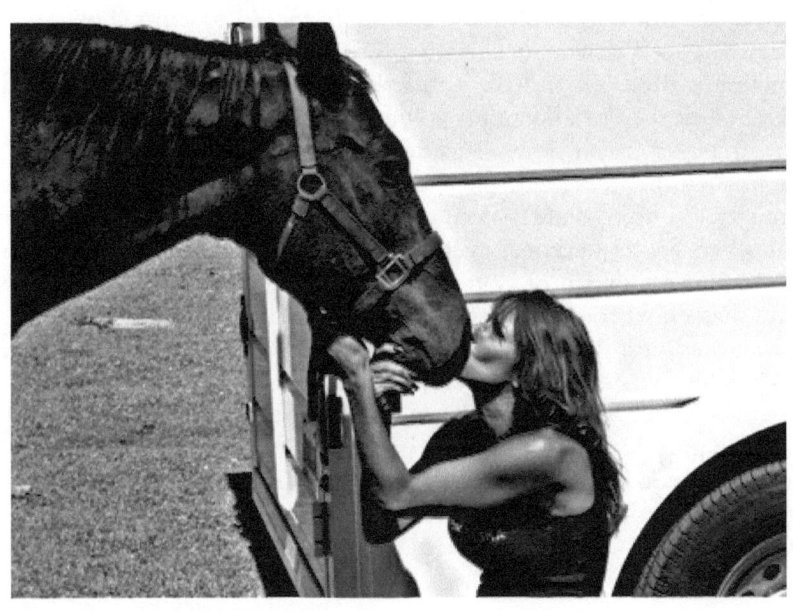

Who Said So?

Any new adventure opens up an opportunity for everyone to give you their best advice on how to achieve your goals. Owning a horse, while exciting, is hard work. Unlike "pet" ownership, there is a lot more to lose if you make an error, like your very well being to the extent of losing consciousness. Everyone seems to know the best way to train a horse, interpret a horse's behavior and have the answers to your inexperience causing problems. Early on in my rides with my own horse, I became so overwhelmed with so many voices telling me which technique is the best, and bless their hearts, their analysis of my applied skills (or lack thereof). Wanting to be a proficient rider and respecting so many opinions, it can be hard to decipher just who's advice to apply. I have learned the horse and rider relationship is all about connection and chemistry. Your horse feels you; he feels every heartbeat that pops out of chest when you're nervous, every turning of your stomach when you're upset, and every twitch of your limbs when you're anxious, all before you realize that's how you're feeling. With this in mind, it is equally important for you, the rider, to feel your horse's every movement and action before it begins the unstoppable process of reactionary behavior that can be dangerous to the both of you. Just as in life, there are many experts, but trust your inner voice and connect with what it is that is best for you. To react with action because the experts say, can result in a disconnect between your mind and soul and result in an unnecessary battle between peace and consciousness.

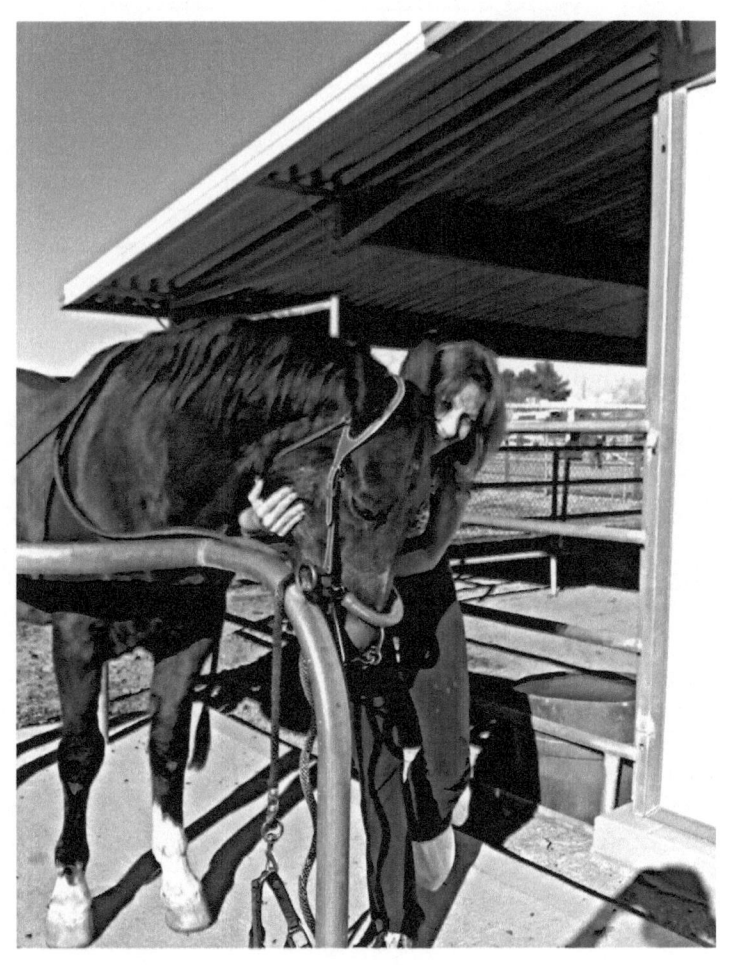

Who's Really in Control?

Novice rider or not, I have always loved horses, and not just in that every girl loves horses way. I ascribe more to what they call "Natural Horsemanship," which in my terms means there is never a need to be mean to your horse (that's not what it really means). My sweet spirited Quarter Horse and I are a match made in heaven! Sure we've had our struggles the first year, but I spoiled him, pampered him, and given the life he had before, made sure he was always treated "good" like the dear friend who rescued him before we met. Things like spurs and bits would not be used with my baby, if I could help it. It's amazing when the battle of the wills ensues and you are confronted with a hairy beast that out-weighs you by 1,000 pounds, how quickly you learn you must remain in control if you want to actually ride your horse or you can be severely injured. Big cuddly lovable animals, though in tune to your bad days and just love on you unconditionally, are still BIG ANIMALS with animal tendencies. They can be unpredictable, toss their weight around, and have bad days and bad attitudes. When they throw a tantrum, it typically involves throwing you....several feet...in the air...until finally in your decent, you find yourself stopping gracelessly on the ground, if you're lucky. There are much worse scenarios, like being dragged by a horse, trampled by a horse, kicked by a horse. Oh the stories I've heard are endless and certainly taught me respect for what it is I am doing up there. How is this in any way related to life? I am in control of my own life; every little turn, is dictated by me; unless of course I let the big hairy beast called life, control me.

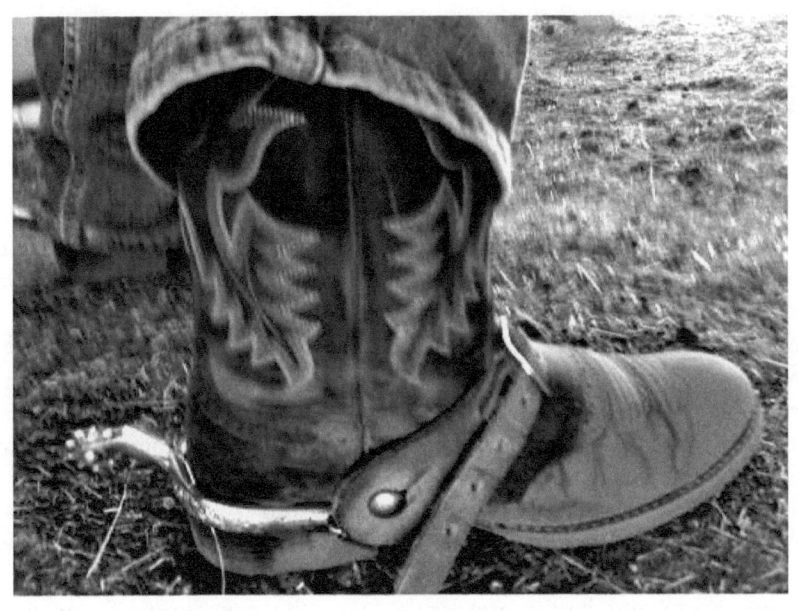

Get Outta Dodge

A wonderful experience with your horse is what they call "Trailering Out." Some horses, like Jr get barn-sour, so leaving for a ride in a trailer tends to be a more pleasurable ride. I've heard when you put them in a trailer and leave familiar surroundings; they simply don't have that run home mentality. With Jr, I have found this to be true. I did learn, however, though they may not attempt to turn back and go home, they somehow know where they started, and that becomes home. While out with a friend exploring a new trail, we encountered an interesting scenario. While passing the backyards of several newly built homes in an attempt to get to a mountain trail, a rather large black and white Great Dane we'll call "Woof" made a surprise appearance. We were protected by a concrete wall, but, nonetheless, Cali, (my friend's horse) who was several feet ahead of me, completely freaked out when "Woof" rushed the wall barking furiously. Cali started jumping, backing up and doing common spooked horse behaviors. At the same time, a very noisy garbage truck was coming up the road which intensified the perceived threat to the horses' environment. Terri, my friend, was doing a great job getting Cali under control. Jr, well, he was watching all this and basically said, "Oh Hell NO!" and turn around and started running back towards the trailer. Terri and I just laughed as I am sure we looked ridiculous. I got Jr calmed down on the side of the trail, and we waited for Terri and Cali to catch up. Recognizing why he felt threatened, I let him run away a little from the whole scene. After we were all calmed down, we took another route and had a great ride (with the exception of one uphill battle).

Ordinarily, you shouldn't let your horse run away from situations, but there are those times when there is a proposed threat and trying to force your way through perceived and potential danger (or worst just hang out in it) is, in my opinion, just plain stupid. After all, running from our problems doesn't solve them, and we never really work through them when we do. However, there are times when turning your back on what could cause you harm (physically, emotionally, and/or mentally) is necessary for your own well-being and probably for those around you as well. I guess the most important thing to be keen to, is to know the difference between running from a problem because you just don't want to deal with it and being able to identify which situations will impact you in a negatively life altering way if you confront and try to push through it. Some situations, no matter what positivity we try to bring to the situation, will not make any difference except with the self-imposed negative impact we induce. The important things to consider are outside factors like big dogs that can brutally eat you and enormous machinery that can crush you; these things certainly validate a need to run!

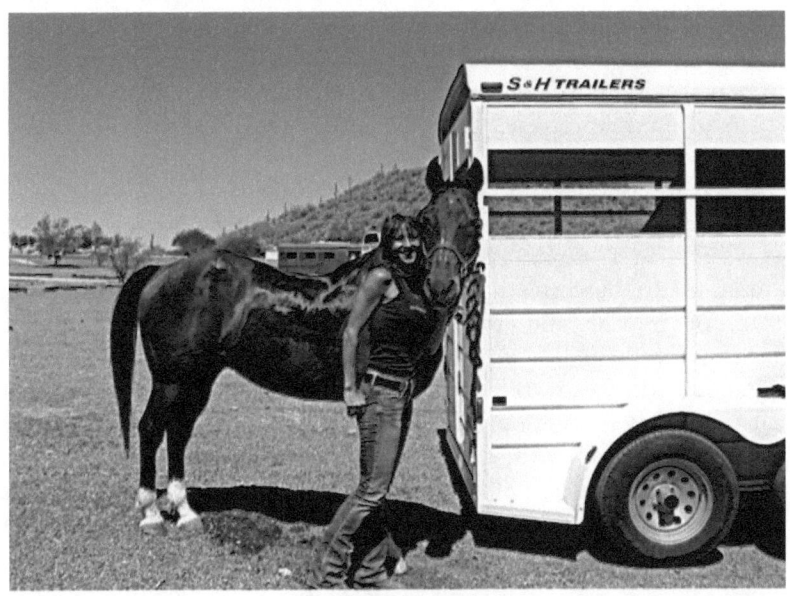

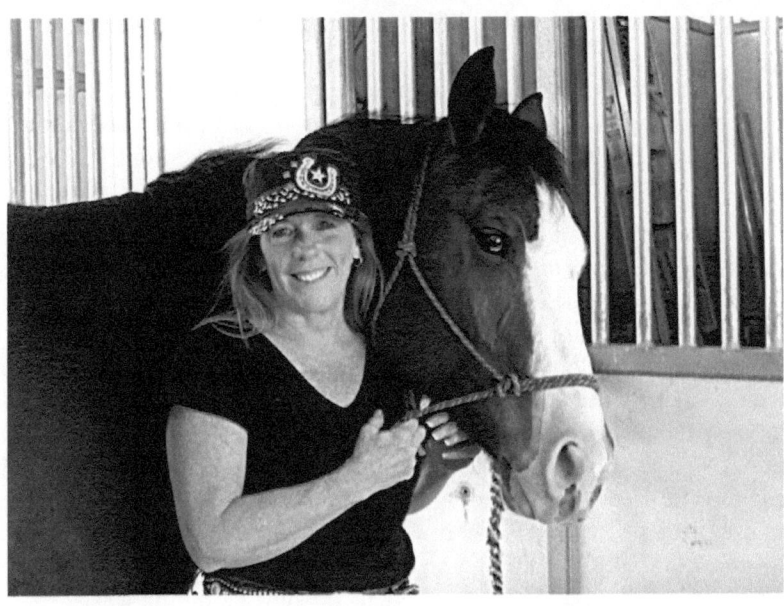

Uphill Battle

On one of Terri and my very beautiful, scenic trail rides, I encountered an uphill battle with Jr. After trailering our horses and surviving our "get outta dodge" experience with Woof, we found our way to an actual designated trail to some of the most beautiful scenery that makes Arizona my preferred place of residence. While we were taking in the sites and baking in the sun, we approached a big rocky hill we were determined to conquer, but first we decided it was a good time to stop and hydrate with a water break. We did our thing for a minute, drank some water, had a smoke, laughed about Woof and let our horse have a few minutes to contemplate the feat before us. I'm thinking this was a mistake for Jr. Cali and Terri started up the hill, and it was pretty uneventful for them. It was pretty uneventful for me and Jr as well, meaning, he didn't want to move. He took one look at that rocky hill and articulated clearly though unable to speak that he just isn't going to do it. He wasn't being stubborn, but he was being a brat. Sometimes I am convinced he just messes with me to get a reaction. Oh, he got a reaction. As much as I hate the thought of using spurs, this ride was this first time I had to actually use them to "spur him on." When I say actually use them, that didn't mean I had to just rest them on him to make him aware I have them; I had to lift my leg and kick him with them (though I was still gentle). It's kind of like the difference between mom showing you the wooden spoon and feeling the impact of the wooden spoon after seeing her wind up and swing it. We did get up the hill just fine, and it was a lot of fun after we got started, for both me and Jr I'm pretty confident had we not stopped, he would have kept going and there would not have been a need to spur him on to get up that hill.

Mountains and valleys are a part of our everyday life. Stopping at the foot of a hill can sometimes be a good time to renew your energy. Most of the time though, not unlike Jr when we stop; we find it harder to get a good start heading up that hill. We look at the mountain before us, contemplate our options and find it easier to just stay in the valley. Jr and I made it up that hill, at first it was a little rocky and unsure footed, but once we gained a little momentum the climb got easier. The view was amazing even at the halfway point, and Jr managed just fine; actually, I'm pretty sure he had a good time too. If you missed the point, no matter what uphill battle you face, do not stop and stare at it just keep moving forward, even if you're footing is unsure. One step at a time, not only will you get to the top; you will be amazed at the view along the way.

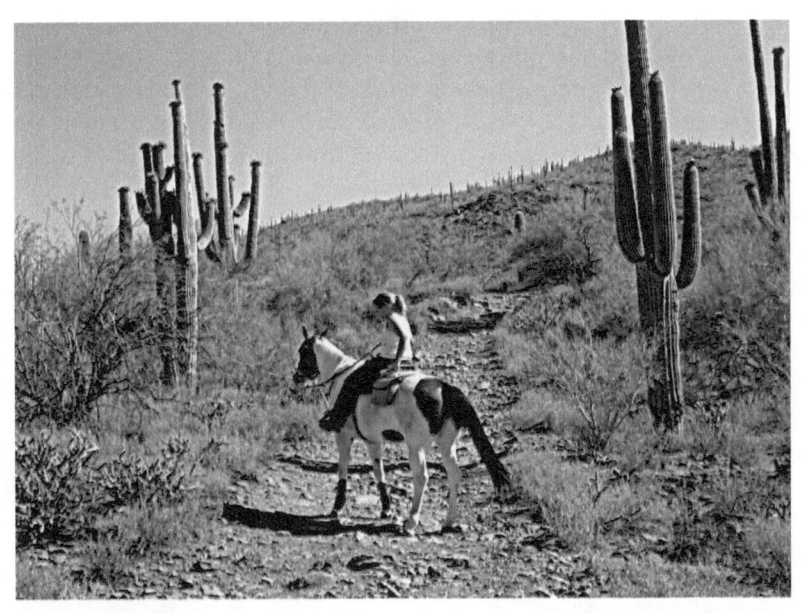

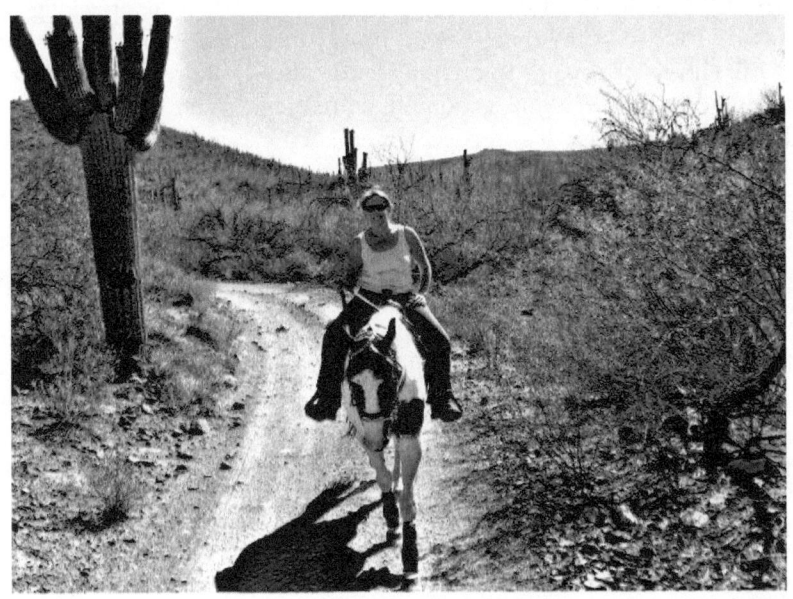

On The Other Side

After surviving "Woof" and conquering the "Uphill Battle" we found ourselves on the other side. The other side is wonderful place to be! Jr worked hard that day; it was Memorial Day and quite memorable it was. It was hot, a new experience and filled with moments that challenged us, got the adrenaline flowing and made us laugh. The entire trip was three or four hours, but we created some really good memories. After a ride whether you trailer it or ride in the arena at home, my first lesson is applied every time without fail: never put your horse away dirty. This means, no matter how tired you are, you must groom him, brush him, clean his frogs (hoofs) and my favorite part, though this is not necessary, with a wet paper towel wipe out his eyes and clean out his nose. This is my favorite part because it is where I taught Jr how to "kiss" me back when I kiss his muzzle. After doing this when you trailer out, you then load them up and take them home. The ride was amazing and we made it back to the other side of the mountain! You would think that was enough, but we had more work to do. After grooming, loading them up, driving them back and unpacking the trailer, we hosed off the horses, groomed them again, fed them, cleaned out there water buckets, filled them, parked the trailer, unhooked the trailer, and finally, after that, sat down. Oh, loading and unloading a trailer for a ride is like packing up a family of four to go camping. You must take saddles, tack (that's what they call all the stuff you use on your saddle, headstall, reins, just anything your horse may need), your grooming equipment, water for your horse, a little feed just in case it's needed, emergency care items, and of course anything the humans might need. One more thing, horse treats; I always make sure we have "cookies." If it sounds like a lot of work it is! It's logical that on your way out that it isn't really that much work, probably because of the excitement you feel going on the ride. But when you are on the other side of that mountain and you achieve a good ride, why does it seem like more work than before the ride? Maybe because you get tired out from everything good and challenging in going uphill and the reward of getting over it to the other side gives you the false sense of completion. Isn't that the truth about life; we overcome one uphill battle and make it to the other side only to discover there is another mountain in your view.

All the work before and after every trail ride really is worth the effort, the memories you create in the journey are irreplaceable, and the lessons you learn make you who you are. I have learned to enjoy every aspect of horse ownership and take in each moment with a fresh perspective that it is like no other moment I've had or ever will have again.

When you get to the other side, take it all in. Appreciate where you've been and what you've become; it is unlike anything before or after that moment and you've earned the right to enjoy it. You will do it all over again, but no need to worry about that moment. It will come with a new adventure, more memories and yet another life lesson. The journey is never really complete because no one really knows what's on the other side until we get there. We are all on the other side of one mountain or another. Maybe one day we will all arrive at the same place at the same time. I suppose that's our hope in death; that we will all be at our final destination together. If that be true, come what may, no matter who arrives first, I will see you on the other side.

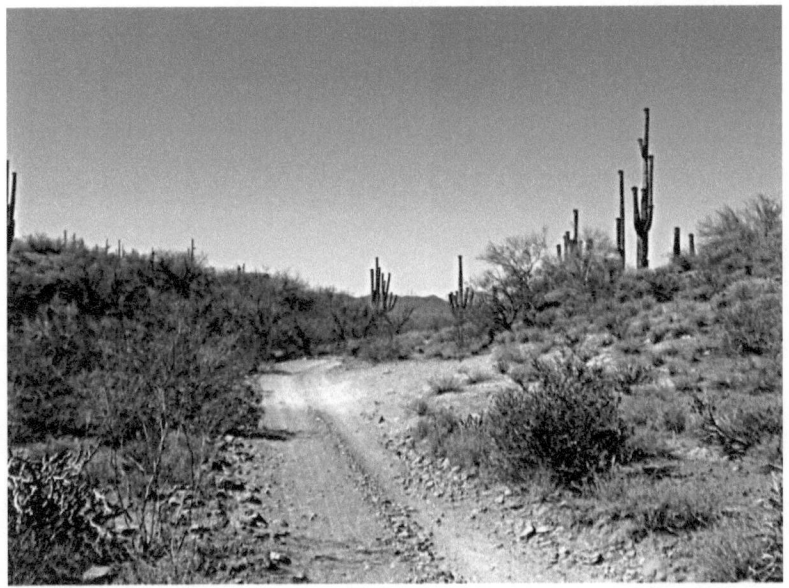